Here's what people are saying about this book:

"The Minnesota Job Seeker's Sourcebook is required reading for all of my clients. Nothing compares with its detail and accuracy. The time and energy saved by using this guide makes it an essential tool for job seekers and career changers. Buy it and use it."

—*Kevin J. Nutter, Ph.D., Program Director*
Career Development Center, University of Minnesota

"The new statewide Minnesota Job Seeker's Sourcebook is a must-have reference guide for anyone seeking a job. It's right on target, complete and thorough, characterized by a real understanding of the reader's needs."

—*Brian Anderson, Editor*
MPLS.ST.PAUL Magazine

"Hailed as a groundbreaking resource when first published, this revised edition of the Minnesota Job Seeker's Sourcebook is an indispensible tool for job seekers and the people who help them."

—*John Eckberg, President*
Minnesota Career Development Association

"The Minnesota Job Seeker's Sourcebook is about bridging the gap between yesterday's pink slip and tomorrow's new job. It's about tapping resources and taking action. It's about linking job seekers with real questions to experts with real answers. It's about helping people get hired."

—*Hal Freeman, Chairman*
Job Transition Support Group, Colonial Church of Edina

"The Minnesota Job Seeker's Sourcebook is your first stop in your job hunt. This practical guidebook makes quick work of linking you to the employment experts you need to succeed."

—*Melanie Keveles, Co-author*
Fired For Success: How to Turn Losing Your Job Into the Opportunity of a Lifetime

Here's what people are saying about this book:

"This user-friendly guidebook is a power-packed toolbox that quickly sets job seekers on the road to employment."
—*Tom Norman, Director*
Dakota County Employment and Training Center

"Not just another cut and paste list of outdated phone numbers, the Minnesota Job Seeker's Sourcebook is the best job-search book for resource information you can use, and advice that makes sense."
—*Mark Gisleson, Founder*
Minnesota Resume Network

"Whether hiring or downsizing, the Minnesota Job Seeker's Sourcebook is a 'must' on the desks of Minnesota employers. During a workforce reduction, this guide—with its thorough introduction to job-seeking resources—is a reassuring and practical tool for affected employees."
—*Mary Jo Ready, Dislocated Worker and Employer Liaison*
Employers Association, Inc.

"For accurate listings of local job-seeking resources, the Minnesota Job Seeker's Sourcebook is your one-stop shop."
—*Robert Riskin, Author*
Between Opportunities: A Survival Guide For Job Seekers and Career Changers

"The Minnesota Job Seeker's Sourcebook is one of the most comprehensive resources I've seen for job seekers. We recommend it highly to our clients."
—*Yvette Oldendorf, President*
Working Opportunities for Women

"Relocating is hard work, but the Minnesota Job Seeker's Sourcebook has proven to be a welcome job-seeking resource for newcomers."
—*Neal Kielar, Director of Marketing*
Greater Minneapolis Chamber of Commerce

MINNESOTA
JOB SEEKER'S
SOURCEBOOK

MINNESOTA
JOB SEEKER'S SOURCEBOOK

THE COMPLETE STATEWIDE GUIDE TO JOB-SEEKING SUPPORT SERVICES

Edited by Pati Gelfman

SECOND EDITION

RESOURCE PUBLISHING GROUP, INC.
Minnetonka, Minnesota

Minnesota Job Seeker's Sourcebook
The Complete Guide To Minnesota Job Seeking Support Services

Copyright © 1991, 1994 by Resource Publishing Group, Inc.

All rights reserved. No part of this book may be reproduced in any form or by any means, electronic or mechanical, including photocopying, recording or by any information or retrieval system, without the written permission of the Publisher, except where permitted by law. Making copies of this book, or any portion for any purpose other than your own, is a violation of United States copyright laws.

Library of Congress Cataloging-in-Publication data

Minnesota job seeker's sourcebook : the complete guide to Minnesota
   job hunting support services/edited by Pati Gelfman. — 2nd ed.
      p. cm.
   Includes index.
   ISBN 0-9629615-1-5 : $17.95
      1. Job hunting—Minnesota—Directories.   2. Employment agencies
   —Minnesota—Directories.   I. Gelfman, Pati.
   HF5382 . 75. U62M64   1994
   331 . 12 '8 '025776—dc20   93-48511
                                                                      CIP

Cover design: Jonathan Gelfman, Minneapolis, MN

Second Edition, First Printing   1994
PRINTED IN THE UNITED STATES OF AMERICA

Resource Publishing Group, Inc.
P.O. Box 573
Hopkins, Minnesota 55343 USA

Limits of Liability and Disclaimer
The included material was compiled based on information provided to the Publisher. The Publisher assumes no responsibility for errors, inaccuracies, omissions, or any other kind of inconsistency herein. Any slights against people or organizations are unintentional. Publisher makes no warranty of any kind, expressed or implied, with regard to the instructions and suggestions contained in this book. It is sold with the understanding that the Publisher is not engaged in rendering legal, accounting, counseling or any other professional service including employment placement services. If legal advice or other professional assistance is required, the services of a competent and appropriately credentialed professional should be sought.

In loving memory of my parents
Annette and Leon Cook
Who were forever bright and happy
Industrious and hard-working
Who accepted life's pain
Lived life to its fullest
And who firmly believed
That dreams
Are meant to be reached.

PSG

*Other Career Resources
by Resource Publishing Group Inc.*

JOB SEARCH RESOURCE SERIES—The best and most powerful job seeker's information series designed as a practical outplacement benefit for transitioning employees. Minnesota and national editions available.

TWIN CITIES JOB SEEKER'S CALENDAR—Colorful month-at-a-glance poster calendar that quickly directs job seekers to upcoming activities important to their job hunt: job-search classes, workshops, job fairs, networking events, job support group meetings, and much more. Available to career transition agencies, public libraries, and other organizations by annual subscription.

JOB SEEKER'S SURVIVAL KIT—Two practical job-search resources— the Minnesota Job Seeker's Sourcebook, and one month's issue of the Twin Cities Job Seeker's Calendar— for a quick start to a productive job hunt. Available only from Resource Publishing Group.

We welcome your interest in our career publications and custom publishing services.

Please call Resource Publishing Group at (612) 545-5980.

ACKNOWLEDGMENTS

Improving on the award-winning first edition of the Minnesota Job Seeker's Sourcebook was a monumental challenge. But this expanded edition, with a new look, new chapters, and 1,000 job-search resources located throughout Minnesota and western Wisconsin, is testimony to the professionalism, insight, dedication, and skills of our editorial research and design team. I'd like to thank these individuals for a job well done.

Donna Campbell, B.A., Counseling Psychology, University of Minnesota. Donna's extensive experience as a career counselor, and as marketing director at Resource Publishing Group, lent thoughtful enhancements to this book and practical job-seeking tips.

Donna M. Wallace, M.S., Vocational Rehabilitation, University of Wisconsin. St. Paul trainer and career consultant, Donna helped us chart our course for this revised edition, meticulously researched new Twin Cities resources, and contributed resourceful ideas.

Anna Simon, B.A., International Relations/Environmental Studies, U.W.-Madison. Administrative/editorial assistant at Resource Publishing, whose attention to detail and ability to balance a dozen projects at once made updating this book a breeze.

Tami Ruden, B.A., English, University of Minnesota. Administrative manager at Resource Publishing Group, Tami singlehandedly tracked down new resources in central Minnesota and western Wisconsin—and added a spark of enthusiasm to the process.

Linda Saline, 3012 E. First St., Duluth, MN 55812, (218) 724-4932, is an organizational consultant who specializes in team building, interpersonal communications, and supervisory management. Between her busy schedules teaching at major corporations and Wisconsin Indianhead Technical College, Linda exhaustively researched northern Minnesota resources.

Nancy Abel, B.A., English, Mount Mary College, is an accomplished artisan who has also taught job-seeking skills at area colleges. Nancy applied her expertise researching job-seeking resources in southern Minnesota.

Jonathan Gelfman, graphic designer, B.F.A., College of Associated Arts, is responsible for our cover and book design, and meticulously planned (and creatively completed) all desktop production.

I would also like to thank those in the community who encouraged and informed us. Thanks to: Tom Norman, John Eckberg, Caron Hassen, Hal Freeman, Warren Oslin, Mary Larkin, Donald Saynor, Mark Gisleson, Mary Jo Ready, Leo Bright, and Dorothy Johnson.

To family and friends who offered support and encouragement: Ruth Gelfman, Dorothy and Ted Papermaster, Susie, Tzi, Allon and Orlee Tatarka, Barb Clayman, Gail and Al Bender, and Amy Lewis.

To my children, Anna and Jesse Simon, Mike, Jon, Judy and Dan Gelfman who contributed wonderful ideas to this project and who generously lent a helping hand when needed.

And finally to my husband, Buddy (Mark), who was my inspiration; who encouraged this effort; who listened patiently for hours—even though it meant occasionally missing the Viking's kick-off. Who brainstormed and problem-solved and remained constantly positive. My thanks, and my love.

Pati Gelfman
Publisher

Contents

INTRODUCTION   **13**

HOW TO USE THIS BOOK   **15**

CHAPTER ONE
GETTING STARTED   **17**

CHAPTER TWO
GOVERNMENT EMPLOYMENT SERVICES   **27**

CHAPTER THREE
FOR FOCUSING YOUR JOB HUNT   **47**

   CAREER & JOB SEARCH COUNSELING SERVICES   50
     Non-Profit organizations

   CAREER & JOB SEARCH COUNSELING SERVICES   75
     Private Sector

   RESUME PREPARATION SERVICES   87

   SCHOOL CAREER CENTERS   100

   RESEARCH RESOURCES   122

CHAPTER FOUR
WHERE TO FIND EMPLOYMENT LEADS 127
- JOB HOTLINES 128
- SEARCH FIRMS & EMPLOYMENT AGENCIES 145
- RECRUITMENT PUBLICATIONS 161
- JOB LEAD SERVICES 169

CHAPTER FIVE
FOR NETWORKING & SUPPORT 175
- JOB SUPPORT GROUPS 176
- NETWORKING ORGANIZATIONS 186
- HELPLINES & CRISIS REFERRALS 195
- RESOURCES FOR MEETING BASIC NEEDS 206

CHAPTER SIX
FOR EMPLOYMENT ALTERNATIVES 215
- CONTRACT & TEMPORARY EMPLOYMENT SERVICES 216
- RESOURCES FOR BUYING OR STARTING A BUSINESS 230
- CAREER-MINDED VOLUNTEER AGENCIES 240
- RELOCATION RESOURCES 245
- RETIREMENT PLANNING SERVICES 252
- SCHOOLS & TRAINING CENTERS 254

GLOSSARY 271

INDEX 275

INTRODUCTION

For Job Seeking in a Changing Workplace

At first glance, job seekers today have it all. Education. Experience. Credentials. Why is it then that for many, the job hunt feels like an exercise in futility? Why do some job seekers get lost in the process and disillusioned with the results?

Why? Because these days a productive job quest begins with the alignment of resources—the people, places and things needed to proceed with competence and confidence. Until now, these resources were scattered among dozens of lists and directories. Until now, finding out where to seek guidance and support involved as much time and energy as finding a job.

Now, this award-winning guidebook covers everything you need to know about where to find hundreds of job-hunting support services in Minnesota and western Wisconsin. Here's how to reach the experts and specialists who will help you focus your job search, locate employment leads, tap support networks and explore career alternatives.

The Minnesota Job Seeker's Sourcebook provides up-to-date listings for career and job-search counseling services, government employment programs, resume preparers, employment agencies and search firms, job support groups, networking organizations, job hotlines, job banks, and resume referral services. You will also find resources for early retirement planning, relocation, crisis assistance, interim health care, budget counseling, training and education, self-employment, career-minded volunteering, and more.

And because a growing number of job seekers are (1) those who are unemployed due to economic conditions or corporate downsizing, (2) recent college graduates facing a tight job market, (3) midlife career changers, or (4) individuals who have experienced a job transition before, many listings are included which address the specific needs of these groups.

This book is intended to be a practical, hardworking resource. In this new statewide edition, we have tried to represent a broad sampling of services reflecting a variety of specialties, industries, geographic locations, and levels of affordability.

To our knowledge, no other directory in the country offers such an extensive variety of local resources to the job seeker. We hope that this information leads you to those who can offer you advice or solutions which, in turn, will lead you to your dream job.

To your success.

How To Use This Book

This completely revised and expanded edition of the Minnesota Job Seeker's Sourcebook is an information clearinghouse that will introduce you to hundreds of local employment experts, job-lead sources, retraining opportunities, and transition assistance. Now you can quickly tap resources and take action that may lead you to your next job or new career.

But every job seeker is unique. Every reader will pick up this book with different needs, or at a different point in the job-search process. For that reason, chapters have been designed to be used in random order. Consult the chapter which best addresses your immediate needs, but please review every section for new ideas.

In this new edition, we have expanded our listings to include services located throughout Minnesota and western Wisconsin. In most chapters, we have grouped listings by geographic location: Twin Cities (seven-county metro area), Northern Minnesota, Central Minnesota, Southern Minnesota, and Western Wisconsin.

The first four chapters of this guide contain resources specific to job hunting. Chapter Five shows you where to turn for advice, support, and "people connecting" during your job transition. Chapter Six introduces resources for interim solutions and career alternatives. Each listing tells you how to contact the organization, what services to expect, who is eligible, how to apply, and fee information.

Happy hunting.

CHAPTER ONE

Getting Started

By virtue of picking up this book, chances are good you are:

✔ Recently out of a job;

✔ Exploring a new career direction or job change;

✔ Seriously entering the job market for the first time;

✔ Re-entering the job market after a long absence, or

✔ Planning a move to Minnesota or Wisconsin.

Your first assignment is to get organized. Here are some quick tips to help you launch a productive job quest.

APPLY FOR UNEMPLOYMENT INSURANCE.

If you've lost your job through no fault of your own, you may be eligible for unemployment insurance. Apply immediately. Unemployed persons receive weekly payments up to 26 weeks, with occasional extensions. The size of the check and number of payments depend on past employment and wages prior to losing your job.

If you're entitled to unemployment insurance, use it. Don't let your pride get in the way. This interim income will soften the financial blow of losing your job, and allow you to put efforts into job seeking. Apply at the Job Service office nearest you (see Chapter Two for locations). Expect your first check to arrive in about three weeks.

FIND INSURANCE COVERAGE.

Try to maintain health insurance during this stressful time. COBRA is a federal law which allows you, under certain circumstances, to continue to buy group health care coverage from your former employer for 18 months, at up to 102 percent of the group rate. Research your alternatives. While you were working, your employer probably paid a portion on your monthly premium—and the full cost may come as a shock. It may be cheaper to arrange for health coverage through your spouse's plan. Some insurance companies may also offer short-term plans. If you opt for COBRA coverage, sign the necessary paperwork promptly.

If your company-paid life insurance policy is discontinued, purchase an inexpensive term policy, especially if you have a family to protect. (For information on interim health care, see Chapter Five.)

CUT YOUR EXPENSES.

Make an accounting of your household financial standing. Add up your income, including any severance pay you've received, then deduct your expenses. Look for short-term spending cuts. Try to reduce spending on restaurant meals, dry cleaning, cable TV, long-distance telephone calls, house cleaning help, newspaper and magazine subscriptions, or health club memberships. You may benefit from budget counseling to keep your household on track.

BE PREPARED FOR AN EMOTIONAL ROLLER COASTER.

Job transition is one of life's major stresses. Expect to feel a gamut of emotions, like shock and disbelief, anger, depression, despair—even periods of elation. A job support group can help you and your family members accept your situation and move forward. Financial crisis can further strain an already difficult time. Seek professional help, if needed. (See listings, Chapter Five.)

GETTING STARTED

FOCUS YOUR JOB HUNT.

If you don't know where you're headed, how will you get there? Now is the time to identify your unique talents, clarify your career goals, and set up a strategy to find the job you want. Your efforts in focusing may actually shorten your job hunt. And employers are impressed by applicants with a confident sense of direction.

Read career guides. Attend job seeking workshops. Get help from one of the hundreds of career or job-search counseling services provided by government, non-profit or private agencies. (See Chapters Two and Three for listings.)

THINK ABOUT INTERIM EMPLOYMENT.

Strapped? No severance? Consider free-lance, contract, or temporary employment to ease financial stress while you're hunting for your first-choice job. An interim job can also help you learn new skills, stay professionally active, and network within a new organization. If you're receiving unemployment benefits, check with a Job Service representative about whether temporary employment income will affect your benefits.

CAREER-MINDED VOLUNTEERING.

Utilize your professional or job skills in a volunteer capacity to broaden your professional network, feel good about yourself, learn new skills, and add experience to your resume.

CONSIDER YOUR OPTIONS.

A job loss or other unplanned transition motivates some folks to re-think their direction. Now may be the time to go back to school for a quick class, or advanced degree. Maybe you want to start a business. Relocate in a new community with brighter job prospects. Or, examine the pros and cons of early retirement. Research your options.

Job Seeking Tips From The Experts

We sought out career development experts and asked them for their best job seeking ideas. Here are some of their suggestions:

❝Don't keep your job hunt a secret. Most jobs come from networking. Everyone you know—or can meet—is a potential job lead. Start with your circle of friends and acquaintances, then expand your network. Keep in touch every four to six weeks or your contacts may assume that you've already landed a job."

❝Avoid non-productive household routines. Arise early and schedule your daily job-search efforts. Target a certain number of interviews you want to achieve each week or month. Keep track of your contacts in a card file. Use a daily planner for appointments and things to do."

❝Don't go through your job hunt alone. Build a support system for yourself without relying exclusively on your spouse or family. Seek out friends, former co-workers, the family physician, a mental health professional, minister or other clergy member. Job support groups and networking organizations are also good places to turn to for peer and professional support."

GETTING STARTED

"Be good to yourself. Keep active. Eat healthy. Occasionally treat yourself to something nice. Place anger where it belongs."

"Gather all the job hunting advice you can get. Attend job-search workshops and resume clinics. Read books and recruitment publications. Allow yourself to be mentored by others who have weathered a job hunt. Ask them what worked—and what to watch out for."

"Most people who make hiring decisions don't like slick resumes. Stick to the basics. Keep it simple and direct."

"Don't randomly broadcast your resume to employment agencies and search firms. Most are specialists in certain industries. Find out which firms specialize in your industry or profession. Contact each one directly."

"Thoroughly research potential employers before you apply or interview for a job. Few applicants take the time, and your homework will get noticed. Employers expect you to know, at the very least, who they are and what they do."

"Buy the best suit or dress you can afford for interviewing, even one that's a step above the quality you normally wear. This investment could reduce your job seeking efforts by one week or more."

"If you suspect that you're the first to interview for a job, try to re-schedule. The last person interviewed has a better chance of being hired than the first. If you're offered a choice of Tuesday, Wednesday or Thursday, take Thursday. The worst day to interview is Monday. The worst time to interview is late afternoon."

MINNESOTA JOB SEEKER'S SOURCEBOOK

❝For job hunters over 50: It's illegal for prospective employers to ask your age, so most won't. During an interview, focus on your career achievements, not on your grandchildren. Avoid using self-defeating statements like: 'When I was your age...' or, 'I may be older than most of your employees, but...' Invest in an updated wardrobe, and keep abreast of technological changes."

❝Send thank-you notes!"

❝During a job interview, make eye contact, especially when making an important point. Employers are more likely to hire candidates who look them directly in the eye. Some interviewers believe that they can read an applicant's personality, confidence, honesty, and sincerity in their eyes."

❝Set high standards when you communicate. Every form of correspondence is a reflection on the quality of your work. Proofread for misspellings, poor grammar and typing errors. Each time you finish a cover letter, read it out loud. Wherever you stumble, or run out of breath, you need to do more work."

❝If your employer offers you an early retirement incentive, look before you leap. The enticing short-term benefit may not outweigh the long-term effect on your future retirement income. Get professional advice before making a decision."

❝Maintain a positive attitude. Henry Ford once said: 'Whether you think you can or you can't, you're right.' Associate only with positive, encouraging people who believe in you."

Living **BETTER** with **LE$$**

Money-saving tips for times of transition

Plan dining-out excursions around coupons and special deals. Early-bird dinners can save you money if you're willing to eat during off-peak hours or on slower days of the week.

Review your insurance policies. Consider raising the deductible on your auto insurance policies. Ask your agent for quotes on combined auto and homeowners policies. Inquire about discounts for non-smokers, non-drinkers, and accident-free drivers.

Job seekers may be able to save up to 75 percent on bus fare with a special Job Seeker's Pass. Passes are available to individuals enrolled in many government-funded jobs programs. If you are enrolled, ask your counselor for details.

Don't forgo cultural events just because you're on a budget. Call local theaters and ask if you can volunteer as an usher or in some other capacity for free admission to the current production. Don't forget about rush seats, and student or alumni discounts.

Weigh the costs and benefits of your current checking and savings accounts. Your financial institution may allow you to switch to a reduced or no-fee account at no charge. Change back to your present program as your financial situation improves.

Set a weekly cash budget and stick to it. Avoid using ATM or credit cards to advance yourself cash. Stay away from gambling casinos.

MINNESOTA JOB SEEKER'S SOURCEBOOK

Museums, zoos, and art galleries offer free-admission days. Don't forget about $1 movies, or renting videos and CDs at the public library. For more low-cost family fun, contact your state department of tourism and request a schedule of upcoming community events and festivals. Many offer free attractions and entertainment.

Clipping and using store coupons can make an astounding difference in your grocery bill. Regularly check Sunday circulars. If you find a particularly valuable coupon on an item you regularly use, ask friends or relatives to save their circulars for you.

Consignment and thrift stores are full of surprises. Update your wardrobe with inexpensive accessories and high quality, gently worn clothing. You may even find new items donated at the end of the season by major retailers.

Living better with less is the theme of several subscription newsletters designed to help you pinch pennies. Some titles are:
Consumer's Best, (612) 929-4604
Tightwad Gazette, RR1, Box 3570, Leeds, Maine 04263
Living Cheap News, Box 700058, San Jose, CA 95170
Cheapskate Monthly, Box 2135, Paramount, CA 90723;
Skinflint News, 1460 Noell Blvd., Palm Harbor , FL 34683
Rat Race Courier, c/o SIMS Inc., P.O. Box 6190, Lancaster, PA 17607.

Publisher overstock companies are great sources of inexpensive gifts. They offer a wide variety of new hard cover and paperback books at deep discounts. If you prefer ordering by mail, send for a free catalog from Edward R. Hamilton, Falls Village, CT 06031-5000.

Scour your closets, workroom, garage, and junk drawers for new, unused items—wiper blades, spray paint, photo refill pages, clothing, etc. Return them to the store where purchased for cash or credit. Many stores accept returns (even on purchases made eons ago) without a receipt, as long as the store name appears on the price sticker.

GETTING STARTED

The students at local technical colleges need to practice their new skills, so many training centers offer a variety of student-provided services to the public—at incredible savings. Enjoy a gourmet meal, receive a pampering facial or massage, get your car repaired, buy discounted bakery products, receive a haircut—even have dental work done, all at deeply discounted prices.

Don't deprive yourself of the opportunity to attend professional conferences and meetings. Some organizations let potential members attend a few meetings before joining. Others offer reduced or deferred fees to unemployed members.

Your junk may be someone's treasure. Look through collections of records, CDs, baseball cards, military clothing, sports equipment, collectibles, antiques, and old books. Collectors and second-hand stores may pay for your items. Before parting with valuable items, have them appraised.

Before you make a trip to the local aluminum can recycler, check your workshop, basement, and garage for metal scraps and wire. Quick extra cash awaits you.

Treat yourself to a beauty makeover. To promote their products and services, department stores often offer makeovers with free cosmetics or perfume samples. Resist the urge to purchase now. As your cash flow improves, you can return the favor.

Ask your local utility company to conduct an energy audit. They will provide you with tips on reducing consumption and making your home more energy efficient. Close off rooms when not in use. Reduce the water heater temperature setting.

Review your association membership benefits. Now may be the time to utilize their group discount programs for eye wear, emergency road service, insurance, and discount buying clubs.

GOVERNMENT EMPLOYMENT PROGRAMS

The range of services offered by the Job Service varies depending on the size of the community, staff, available resources, and case loads. If the Job Service cannot meet your needs, they will refer you to other agencies.

FOR VETERANS ONLY

Veterans, by law, have a right to priority treatment at the Job Service. After registering at the Job Service office, a veteran should ask to see the veterans representative or the Disabled Veteran's Outreach Program Representative (DVOP). These representatives ensure that vets receive preferential treatment. Local veterans representatives and DVOPs are also available at locations other than the Job Service. For more information, call the Job Service office.

Veterans also have re-employment rights which are protected by the Veterans Re-employment Rights Department, a division of the Veterans Employment and Training Service (VETS). Veterans and employers alike often have questions about these rights. For specific information, call the veteran's organizations listed at the end of this chapter.

Government-Funded Employment Programs

> *Before I lost my job, I made $55,000 a year. I certainly never thought I would qualify for government-funded job-search counseling. Besides, even if I did, I was sure that the quality of the services would be second-rate.*

Life can be full of surprises.

Robert C. (not his real name), a 46-year-old executive had never lost a job before. He had never applied for unemployment benefits. And he had certainly never turned to the government for employment assistance. But that was before he was laid off from a $55,000 a year job. Though he attended a two-day outplacement workshop provided by his employer, he was immediately thrust into a highly competitive job market.

After eight months without finding a job (his unemployment benefits had run out after six months), Robert and his wife began to fall behind on the mortgage payments on their $180,000 home. Discouraged and seriously concerned, he learned about a government-funded program called EDWAAA (Economic Dislocation & Worker Adjustment Assistance Act).

GOVERNMENT EMPLOYMENT PROGRAMS

EDWAAA is an employment assistance program designed for, among others, workers who have lost their jobs due to layoffs. Robert applied to the program, was accepted, and began to meet weekly with a job counselor at a suburban Job Service office.

The counselor had experience working with career track professionals. She helped Robert re-focus his resume, sharpen interviewing skills, and consider new places to market himself. Her encouragement helped renew his confidence, and he began to invest more energy into job seeking. Six weeks later, he found a job.

Not all EDWAAA participants (or those of other employment programs) find such a tidy solution to their unemployment. But Robert is the first to admit that he was pleasantly surprised to qualify for this government help. Like so many unemployed executives with six-figure assets *but no current earned income*, he believed that he had nowhere to turn. Fortunately he was wrong.

The government has passed many laws authorizing and funding programs to help unemployed and underemployed people. Some are designed to help those who are laid off through no fault of their own; others are designed to upgrade levels of employment. All help define job goals and strategies, and develop job-seeking techniques. Many provide job leads and on-going support during the employment transition.

Federal and state governments generally contribute funds to these programs. But government agencies are not always the actual providers of services. Many providers are neighborhood social service agencies or employment centers.

To receive help from these government programs first requires that you apply. If you are unprepared, this can be a bureaucratic nightmare. Still you don't have to be an expert on every program to find help.

MINNESOTA JOB SEEKER'S SOURCEBOOK

We have found that simply knowing which program names to drop and, in a broad sense, what the eligibility requirements are, can help to cut through red tape.

When talking with an intake counselor, ask about specific programs by name. Explain why you think you're eligible. This should be enough to get someone's attention to potentially qualify you for the service. At the very least, this approach will get your questions answered faster.

On the following pages, the Minnesota Job Seeker's Sourcebook has described several common government-funded programs. If you find one you think you might be eligible for, look in the margin for a large symbol—diamond, triangle, square, etc. Then skim through Chapters Two and Three of this book, looking for matching symbols, found next to the listings for community and government employment services. You can expect that these organizations provide the program you are interested in. Contact the organizations after reading their descriptions in this book. Remember: Many can only serve clients who work or live in a specific geographic area or neighborhood.

If you are in doubt about who to contact, call an organization close to your home. Don't worry. Most are well-practiced in fielding phone calls and will refer you to the appropriate place.

PLEASE NOTE: Even though you may be eligible to receive government-funded services, you may have to wait a long time to receive assistance—or you may never receive assistance at all. These programs are only offered as long as funds are available. With so many job seekers in need of assistance, funds can and do run out at various agencies.

GOVERNMENT EMPLOYMENT PROGRAMS

The programs listed below are a sampling only of the many government-funded employment programs available.

■ JTPA
Job Training Partnership Act

The Job Training Partnership Act (JTPA) was established by Congress in 1983 to help unemployed and low-income individuals gain necessary skills and find productive employment. Services include coaching in job-seeking skills, aptitude testing, financial aid for training, and job placement. Eligibility is based on income (not assets or former salary), residency, and other criteria.

You may qualify for services if you have little or no income (this may also apply to individuals who are unemployed and whose unemployment benefits have already expired). You may also qualify if you are a dislocated worker, school drop out, older worker (55 or older), handicapped, or are receiving public assistance. There is also funding available for a narrowly defined group of veterans.

◆ EDWAAA
Economic Dislocation & Worker Adjustment Assistance Act

EDWAAA is funded to help people who lose their jobs because of a plant closing, mass layoff, change in technology, or change in the economy. You may be eligible if your unemployment benefits have run out, or it's unlikely you'll find work in your former occupation or industry. You may also be eligible if you are a displaced homemaker, or were self-employed and became unemployed due to economic conditions in your community.

All Job Service offices have some EDWAAA funds, even though it may be a minimal amount. If the Job Service office cannot provide help, ask for referrals to other local service providers who can.

▲ OLDER WORKER PROGRAMS

If you are 55 or older, and meet income and residency guidelines, you may be eligible for employment assistance through a variety of older worker programs. The JTPA Older Worker Program offers skills assessment, counseling, classroom and on-the-job training, and assistance finding a job in the private sector. You also must meet income and residence guidelines.

Senior Community Service Employment Program (SCSEP) helps low-income, older workers find part-time employment in public-sector jobs with senior citizen centers, schools, hospitals, libraries, social service projects and other community projects.

▶ STATE DISLOCATED WORKER PROGRAM

Like EDWAAA, this state-funded program helps individuals who were laid off through no fault of their own. Since 1990, the State of Minnesota has significantly increased funding to this program. Many agencies in addition to Job Service offices, serve Dislocated Workers.

GOVERNMENT EMPLOYMENT PROGRAMS

❖ **STRIDE**
Success Through Reaching Individual Development & Employment

STRIDE is a program to help AFDC recipients receive employment training and ultimately become self-supporting. Caretakers are eligible if they are under age 24 without high school diploma's or equivalences, have little or no work experience, and who will be ineligible for AFDC in two years either due to the age of their youngest child or because they have received AFDC assistance for 36 of the last 60 months.

The program includes vocational counseling and assessment of employment, training, education, and support needs. An important component of STRIDE is the opportunity to participate in work programs.

This chapter continues on the following page.

MINNESOTA JOB SEEKER'S SOURCEBOOK

▲■◆ JOB SERVICE OFFICES

❖❭ If you're looking for work, the Job Service or Department of Jobs and Training offices are the first places to turn. These state-run offices administer unemployment insurance benefits, but also may provide a variety of additional services: access to a computer job bank, employment counseling, interest and ability testing, to name a few.

This office can also determine your eligibility for special government-funded programs which offer more comprehensive career and job-search counseling. Eligibility may surprise you. Some programs are funded specifically to help individuals who have lost their jobs due to layoffs, etc., including those who formerly earned a generous salary. If you think you may be eligible, take a serious look at government Jobs and Training services.

Veterans should ask to meet with a representative who assists vets in receiving priority service. Call for information. No charge for services.

TWIN CITIES

BLAINE
1201 89th Ave. N.E.
Blaine, MN 55434
(612) 785-6450

BLOOMINGTON
9401 James Ave. So.
Bloomington, MN 55431
(612) 948-2000

BROOKLYN PARK
7100 Northland Circle
Brooklyn Park, MN 55428
(612) 536-6000

KING CENTER
270 No. Kent Street
St. Paul, MN 55102
(612) 224-4601

MINNEAPOLIS
1200 Plymouth Ave. No.
Minneapolis, MN 55411
(612) 520-3500

MINNEAPOLIS
777 E. Lake Street
Minneapolis, MN 55407
(612) 821-4000

MINNETONKA
6121 Baker Road
Minnetonka, MN 55345
(612) 945-3600

NORTH ST. PAUL
2098 E. 11th Ave.
No. St. Paul, MN 55109
(612) 779-5666

SHAKOPEE
1137 Shakopee Town Sq.
Shakopee, MN 55379
(612) 496-4160

ST. PAUL
2455 University Ave. W.
St. Paul, MN 55114
(612) 642-0363

STILLWATER
14900 61st St. No.
Stillwater, MN 55082
(612) 297-2440

WEST ST. PAUL
60 E. Marie
W. St. Paul, MN 55118
(612) 552-5000

GOVERNMENT EMPLOYMENT PROGRAMS

GREATER MINNESOTA

ALBERT LEA
916 So. Broadway
P.O. Box 651
Albert Lea, MN 56007
(507) 373-3951

ALEXANDRIA
418 Third Ave. East
Alexandria, MN 56308
(612) 762-7800

AUSTIN
1900 8th Ave. N.W.
Austin, MN 55912
(507) 433-0555

BEMIDJI
1819 Bemidji Avenue
P.O. Box 6007
Bemidji, MN 56601
(218) 755-2936

BRAINERD
1919 So. 6th Street
P.O. Box 767
Brainerd, MN 56401
(218) 828-2450

CAMBRIDGE
1575 E. Hwy. 95
Cambridge, MN 55008
(612) 689-1931

CROOKSTON
721 So. Minnesota St.
Crookston, MN 56716
(218) 281-3593

DETROIT LAKES
801 Roosevelt Avenue
Detroit Lakes, MN 56501
(218) 847-3136

DULUTH
320 W. Second Street
Duluth, MN 55802
(218) 723-4730

DULUTH
4921 Matterhorn Drive
Duluth, MN 55811
(218) 723-4875

EAST GRAND FORKS
1616 Central Ave. N.E.
P.O. Box 666
E. Grand Forks, MN 56721
(218) 773-9841

FAIRMONT
923 No. State Street
Fairmont, MN 56031
(507) 235-5518

FARIBAULT
201 Lyndale Ave. So.
P.O. Box 9
Faribault, MN 55021
(507) 332-3220

FERGUS FALLS
125 W. Lincoln Avenue
P.O. Box 418
Fergus Falls, MN 56538
(218) 739-7560

GRAND RAPIDS
409 13th St. S.E.
P.O. Box 678
Grand Rapids, MN 55744
(218) 327-4480

HIBBING
37th St. & Hwy. 169
P.O. Box 68
Hibbing, MN 55746
(218) 262-6777

HUTCHINSON
P.O. Box 550
Hutchinson, MN 55350
(612) 587-4740

INTERNATIONAL FALLS
407 Fourth Street
Int'l Falls, MN 56649
(218) 283-9427

LITCHFIELD
329 E. Hwy. 12
P.O. Box 1001
Litchfield, MN 55355
(612) 693-2859

LITTLE FALLS
211 S.E. First Street
P.O. Box 120
Little Falls, MN 56345
(612) 632-5427

For an explanation of the symbols on these pages, see pages 33—35.

MINNESOTA JOB SEEKER'S SOURCEBOOK

JOB SERVICE OFFICES, cont.

GREATER MINNESOTA

MANKATO
1650 Madison Avenue
P.O. Box 1210
Mankato, MN 56001
(507) 389-6723

MARSHALL
1424 E. College Drive
P.O. Box 3005
Marshall, MN 56258
(507) 537-6236

MONTEVIDEO
125 So. First Street
Montevideo, MN 56265
(612) 269-8819

MOORHEAD
810 Fourth Ave. So.
Moorhead, MN 56560
(218) 236-2191

MORA
130 So. Park Street
P.O. Box 27
Mora, MN 55051
(612) 679-3611

NEW ULM
1200 So. Broadway
P.O. Box 99
New Ulm, MN 56073
(507) 354-3138

OWATONNA
204 E. Pearl Street
Owatonna, MN 55060
(507) 455-5850

PARK RAPIDS
1011 E. First Street
Park Rapids, MN 56470
(218) 732-3396

RED WING
1606 W. Third Street
Red Wing, MN 55066
(612) 388-3526

ROCHESTER
1200 So. Broadway
P.O. Box 9130
Rochester, MN 55904
(507) 285-7315

ROSEAU
300 S.W. Sixth Street
Roseau, MN 56751
(218) 463-2233

ST. CLOUD
111 Lincoln Ave. S.E.
P.O. Box 67
St. Cloud, MN 56302
(612) 255-3266

ST. CLOUD
P.O Box 67
St. Cloud, MN 56302
(612) 255-2016

THIEF RIVER FALLS
318 No. Knight Avenue
Thief Rr Falls, MN 56701
(218) 681-1100

VIRGINIA
820 No. Ninth Street
Virginia, MN 55792
(218) 749-7704

WADENA
311 Jefferson St. No.
P.O. Box 643
Wadena, MN 56482
(218) 631-3240

WASECA
215 No. State Street
Waseca, MN 56093
(507) 835-5502

WILLMAR
2015 So. First Street
Willmar, MN 56201
(612) 231-5174

WINONA
52 E. Fifth Street
P.O. Box 739
Winona, MN 55987
(507) 453-2920

WORTHINGTON
511 Tenth Street
P.O. Box 159
Worthington, MN 56187
(507) 376-3116

GOVERNMENT EMPLOYMENT PROGRAMS

JOB SERVICE OFFICES
Wisconsin Department of Industry, Labor and Human Relations

WESTERN WISCONSIN

BLACK RIVER FALLS
221 Main Street
Black Rvr Falls, WI 54615
(715) 284-7117

CHIPPEWA FALLS
13 E. Spruce Street
Chippewa Falls, WI 54729
(715) 726-2552

DURAND
317 West Main
Durand, WI 54736
(715) 672-8801

EAU CLAIRE
418 Wisconsin Street
Eau Claire, WI 54703
(715) 836-2901

HAYWARD
111 Main Street
Hayward, WI 54843
(715) 634-4845

HUDSON
516 Second Street
Hudson, WI 54016
(715) 381-5100

INDEPENDENCE
WWTC Career Center
204 Walnut Street
Independence, WI 54747
(715) 985-3392

LA CROSSE
508 Fifth Ave. So.
La Crosse, WI 54601
(608) 785-9341

LA CROSSE JOBS/SAS
118 Mt. Vernon Street
La Crosse, WI 54601
(608) 785-9347

LA CROSSE
WWTC
304 No. Sixth Street
La Crosse, WI 54601
(608) 785-9440

MENOMONIE
1603 Stout Road
Menomonie, WI 54751
(715) 232-4020

PRAIRIE DU CHIEN
429 So. Prairie Street
Prairie du Chien, WI 53821
(608) 326-5545

RICE LAKE
113 North Main
Rice Lake, WI 54868
(715) 234-6826

RIVER FALLS
314 No. Second Street
River Falls, WI 54022
(715) 425-0118

SHELL LAKE
P.O. Box 147
Shell Lake, WI 54871
(715) 468-7155

SIREN
7410 Cty. Road K
P.O. Box 130
Siren, WI 54872
(715) 349-2131

SPARTA
Building B, Route 2
Sparta, WI 54656
(608) 269-8900

SUPERIOR
1616 Tower Avenue
Superior, WI 54880
(715) 392-7800

VIROQUA
123 W. Decker Street
P.O. Box 88
Viroqua, WI 54665
(608) 637-2612

Government
Employment & Training Centers

TWIN CITIES

▲■♦ ANOKA COUNTY JOB TRAINING CENTER
1201 89th Ave. N.E., Suite 235
Blaine, MN 55434
(612) 783-4800   Fax—(612) 783-4844

Open to the public, but eligibility is based on residency, work location or income depending on program. Career planning, job-search counseling, resume development, testing and assessment, training, job leads, referrals to off-site employment programs. Call for appointment. Free.

▲❖ CARVER COUNTY
■♦ EMPLOYMENT AND TRAINING CENTER
600 E. Fourth Street
Chaska, MN 55318
(612) 361-1600

Open to the public, but eligibility is based on residency, work location or income depending on the program. Services include career planning, job-search counseling, resume development. Also provides testing and assessment, training, job leads, and referrals to off-site employment programs. Call for appointment. Free.

■♦ DAKOTA COUNTY
EMPLOYMENT AND TRAINING CENTER
1300 145th St. East
Rosemount, MN 55068
(612) 423-6363

Open to the public, but eligibility is based on residency, income or other criteria determined by program. Services include career planning, job-search coaching, resume development. Also provides assessment, testing, re-training, job leads, referrals to off-site employment programs. Call for appointment. Free.

GOVERNMENT EMPLOYMENT PROGRAMS

HENNEPIN COUNTY DEPARTMENT OF TRAINING AND EMPLOYMENT ASSISTANCE
Hennepin County Government Center
First Level South, 300 So. Sixth Street
Minneapolis, MN 55487
(612) 348-7432—General information
(612) 348-9023—Dislocated Worker Program Info Hotline

Government supervisory agency. Administers funding for broad range of employment programs for residents of suburban Hennepin County (dislocated workers, veterans, people of low income, and families on public assistance), and public jobs for the homeless. Contracts with off-site employment programs.

MINNEAPOLIS EMPLOYMENT AND TRAINING PROGRAM
350 So. Fifth Street, Room 310-1/2 City Hall
Minneapolis, MN 55415
(612) 673-5700

Government supervisory agency. Provides government funding and makes referrals to employment assistance programs offered at neighborhood centers throughout the City of Minneapolis. Programs are free to eligible participants. Eligibility is based on many factors including residency, income, and employment status. Call for information and referrals.

▲❖ RAMSEY COUNTY JOB TRAINING PROGRAM
■◆ Gladstone Community Center
▶ 1945 Manton Street
Maplewood, MN 55109
(612) 770-8900   Fax—(612) 770-6890

Open to the public, but eligibility is based on residency, income, or other criteria determined by program. Services include career planning, job-search coaching, resume and cover letter development. Provides career assessment and testing, training, job leads. Also makes referrals to off-site employment programs. Call for appointment. Free.

For an explanation of the symbols on these pages, see pages 33—35.

41

▲✦■ SCOTT COUNTY HUMAN SERVICES
◆❱ Court House 300
428 So. Holmes Street
Shakopee, MN 55370
(612) 445-7751   Fax—(612) 496-8430

Open to the public, but eligibility is based on residency, work location, or income depending on the program. Services include career planning, job-search coaching, resume development, testing and assessment, training, job leads, placement, educational counseling. Referrals to off-site programs. Call for an appointment. Free.

▲✦■ ST. PAUL EMPLOYMENT & TRAINING CENTER
◆❱ 215 E. Ninth Street
St. Paul, MN 55102
(612) 228-3283   Fax—(612) 292-7981

Open to the public, but eligibility is based on residency, income, employment status or other criteria. Broad range of services including career planning, job search counseling, career testing, training, job leads, resource center. Call for appointment. Free.

▲✦ WASHINGTON COUNTY JOB TRAINING CENTER
■◆ 14900 61st St. No.
Stillwater, MN 55082
(612) 430-6850

Open to the public, but eligibility is based on residency, income or other criteria depending on the program. Services include career planning, assessment and testing. Also provides job-search counseling, resume development, training, job leads, and referrals to off-site employment programs. Call for appointment. Free.

GOVERNMENT EMPLOYMENT PROGRAMS

GREATER MINNESOTA

❖■ DULUTH JOB TRAINING CENTER
332 City Hall
Duluth, MN 55802
(218) 723-3771   Fax—(218) 723-3636

Open only to eligible participants. Services include career assessment and testing, workshops, job bank, resource library, job-search coaching, and job leads. Call for appointment. Free.

❖■ NORTHEAST MINNESOTA OFFICE OF
❖❱ JOB TRAINING
Call for locations in Virginia, Duluth, International Falls, Grand Rapids, Two Harbors, Hibbing, and Cloquet.
820 No. 9th St., Suite 240
P.O. Box 1028
Virginia, MN 55792
(218) 749-1274   Fax—(218) 749-1673

Open only to eligible participants. Services include career assessment and testing, workshops, job bank, resource library, job-search coaching, assistance with resumes and interviews. Drop in. Free.

❖■ STEARNS-BENTON
❖❱ EMPLOYMENT & TRAINING COUNCIL
3333 W. Division, Terrace Level, Suite C
P.O. Box 615
St. Cloud, MN 56302
(612) 656-3990

Open to the public but requirements vary by program. Services include career assessment and testing, workshops, job club, resource library. Also offers job-search coaching, resume and interview preparation. Call for appointment or drop in. Free to those who meet eligibility requirements.

For an explanation of the symbols on these pages, see pages 33—35.

MINNESOTA JOB SEEKER'S SOURCEBOOK

❖■ WINONA DEPARTMENT OF JOBS AND TRAINING
◆❱ 52 E. Fifth Street
▲ Winona, MN 55987
(507) 453-2920

Open to the public but requirements vary by program. Services include career assessment and testing, workshops, job bank, resource library, job-search coaching. Call for appointment. Free.

VETERANS EMPLOYMENT

U.S. DEPARTMENT OF VETERANS AFFAIRS
Vocational Rehabilitation and Counseling Div. (28)
Bishop Henry Whipple Federal Building
Fort Snelling
St. Paul, MN 55111
(612) 725-3165

Open to disabled veterans who qualify for vocational rehabilitation. Services include career planning, assessment, testing, education, training, job placement, personalized counseling. Call for information. Free.

VETERANS RE-EMPLOYMENT RIGHTS
Division of Veterans Employment and Training Service
390 No. Robert Street
St. Paul, MN 55101
(612) 297-1186

Assists military personnel in returning to their pre-military employer. Call for information. Free.

VETERANS EMPLOYMENT AND TRAINING SERVICE
390 No. Robert Street
St. Paul, MN 55101
(612) 296-3665

Administers veterans programs at Job Services. Provides Disabled Veterans Outreach program and Veterans Re-employment Rights.

GOVERNMENT EMPLOYMENT PROGRAMS

SPECIAL NEEDS

STATE SERVICES FOR THE BLIND AND VISUALLY HANDICAPPED
Minnesota Department of Jobs and Training

Call for Minnesota locations.

Twin Cities Metro: (612) 642-0500—Voice
                    (612) 642-0506—TDD
Greater Minnesota: (800) 652-9000—Voice/TDD

Employment assistance service. Open only to visually impaired Minnesota residents. Services include vocational assessment and testing, job placement, job-search coaching, job leads, training, and adjustment counseling. Specializes in rehab technology. Call for appointment. Free.

DIVISION OF REHABILITATION SERVICES
Minnesota Department of Jobs and Training

Call for Minnesota locations.

Twin Cities Metro: (612) 296-5616
Greater Minnesota: (800) 328-9095

Works with individuals with an impairment that is an impediment to employment. Offers vocational assessment and testing, job placement, job-search coaching, job leads, training, and adjustment counseling. Specializes in rehab technology. Call for appointment. Free.

OFFICE OF THE BLIND
Wisconsin Division of Vocational Rehabilitation

Call for Wisconsin locations.
One W. Wilson Street
P.O. Box 7852
Madison, WI 53707
(608) 266-5600

Employment assistance service. Open to visually impaired Wisconsin residents. Services include career assessment, testing, placement, job-search coaching, resume and interviewing assistance. Special equipment for education and on-the-job training. Free.

For an explanation of the symbols on these pages, see pages 33—35.

WISCONSIN DIVISION OF VOCATIONAL REHABILITATION
Wisconsin Department of Health and Social Services

Call for Wisconsin locations.
One W. Wilson Street
P.O. Box 7852
Madison, WI 53707
(608) 266-1281—Voice
(608) 266-9599—TDD

Employment assistance service. Works with individuals with an impairment (physical, mental, cognitive, etc.) that is an impediment to employment. Services include diagnostic evaluation, personal and vocational counseling, restoration, training, placement, follow-up, and post-employment services. Call for information. Free or sliding fee scale.

CHAPTER THREE

FOCUSING YOUR JOB HUNT

Choosing a new career or looking for a job is downright hard work. At times it can be frustrating. At other times insightful. For those who lose their jobs suddenly, or at an advanced age, the job hunt can be a major blow.

If you've been plunged unexpectedly into the job market, now is not the time to put yourself into high gear. Likewise, if you're considering a career change, slow down and focus your job hunt. Understand your strengths and skills. Set goals. Map out strategy. Align your resources before you push ahead looking for a job. Experts claim that the more time you spend focusing on who you are and what you have to offer, the less time you'll spend in your search.

This chapter is your primary road map to the many local people and places who will help you chart your career transition and stay on track. Some of the resources in this section will help you explore your skills, interests, and career goals. Others focus on the specific techniques of the job search. Some full-service organizations do it all.

There are five sections in this chapter: career and job search counseling services in both the non-profit and private sectors, school career centers, resume preparation services, and research resources. We have made a distinction between non-profit and private sector services only to denote the differences in fee structures. Many non-profits offer low-cost services or those available on a sliding fee scale. But, be aware that some career coaches in private practice will also adjust their fees according to your ability to pay.

The qualifications of the professionals listed in this chapter may vary significantly. At the present time, there is no competency-based system for licensing professional career counselors in the State of Minnesota. That means that virtually anyone can be a vocational coach, ready to give advice, suggestions, and directions without having attained any specific training.

This does not mean that there are not hundreds of experienced, highly trained and sincere career professionals in Minnesota. Still, be a savvy consumer. Before you invest in any career-related services, consult the guidelines below.

CONSUMER GUIDELINES FOR SELECTING A CAREER COUNSELOR

Prepared by the National Career Development Association

- Ask the counselor for a detailed explanation of services (career counseling, testing, employment search strategy planning, and resume writing) he or she provides. Make sure you understand the service, your degree of involvement and financial commitment.

- Select a counselor who is professionally trained and will let you choose the services you desire. Make certain you can terminate the services at any time, paying only for services rendered.

- Be skeptical of services that make promises of more money, better jobs, resumes that get speedy results or an immediate solution to career problems.

CAREER & JOB SEARCH COUNSELING SERVICES - NON-PROFIT

- Professional codes of ethics by such organizations as the National Career Development Association, the American Counseling Association, and the American Psychological Association, advise against grandiose guarantees and promises, exorbitant fees, and breaches of confidentiality, among other things.

You may wish to ask for a detailed explanation of services offered, your financial and time commitments, and a copy of the ethical guidelines used by the career counselor you're considering.

For a free copy of "Ethical Standards and Consumer Guidelines" published by the American Counseling Association, call the organization at (800) 347-6647.

Career & Job Search Counseling Services

Non-Profit Organizations

Government funding, along with private foundation grants, makes it affordable for just about everyone these days to take advantage of employment guidance. Career and job-search counseling services offered by non-profit organizations are generally available at a modest rate or on a sliding fee scale.

The services described in this section provide a broad range of resources for the unemployed and underemployed. Some are popular long-standing career programs for women. Others are targeted to minorities, or job seekers with special needs. Many are open to the public but, be advised, you may have to meet eligibility requirements based on income, place of residence, or other criteria.

Expect to get help exploring new careers and honing job-seeking skills. You may also receive job leads, placement services, retraining, and assistance with child care or transportation costs. If you're an executive type, don't expect posh accommodations. While some non-profits are housed in suburban suites, most are tucked into modest, no-nonsense storefronts or neighborhood community centers.

Some non-profit organizations administer government-funded employment programs. See Chapter Two for details, and an explanation of the symbols that precede some of the listings in this chapter.

CAREER & JOB SEARCH COUNSELING SERVICES - NON-PROFIT

TWIN CITIES

A.I.O.I.C. COMMUNITY JOB TRAINING CENTER
1111 Third Ave. So.
Minneapolis, MN 55404
(612) 338-4370   Fax—(612) 338-8862

Services include career assessment, testing, job-search coaching, job club, resource library, job placement, video-taped mock interviews, GED preparation, financial aid assistance. Call for information. Free.

■ AMERICAN INDIAN OIC
1845 E. Franklin Avenue
Minneapolis, MN 55404
(612) 341-3358   Fax—(612) 341-3766

Targeted to Native Americans. Offers job-search coaching, vocational assessment, job bank, GED/basic skills preparation, day care. Also provides training in office skills, casino management, etc. Financial aid available for training programs. Other services are free.

◆■ ANISHINABE COUNCIL OF JOB DEVELOPERS, INC.
❱ 2309 Nicollet Ave. So., Suite 102
Minneapolis, MN 55404
(612) 870-7281   Fax—(612) 870-0017

Targeted to employment needs of Native Americans. Offers career assessment, job-search counseling, resource center, training, job placement and retention. Call for appointment. Free.

CAREER OPPORTUNITIES PREPARATION FOR EMPLOYMENT
Program of Family Service, Inc.

166 E. Fourth St., Suite 200
St. Paul, MN 55101
(612) 222-0311   Fax—(612) 222-8920

Open to the public. Career assessment, testing, job-search coaching, personalized counseling. Call for appointment. Adjusted fee scale.

For an explanation of the symbols on these pages, please see pages 33-35.

❖ CENTER FOR ASIANS AND PACIFIC ISLANDERS
2200 E. Franklin Avenue
Minneapolis, MN 55404
(612) 672-0123   Fax—(612) 672-0125

Serves Southeast Asian, Russian, Caucasian, Middle Eastern, and African refugees. Also provides employment assistance to economically disadvantaged youth and welfare recipients. Provides vocational assessment, job-search coaching, job bank, job club. Free.

▲ CENTER FOR CAREER CHANGE
Division of Metropolitan Senior Federation
1885 University Avenue
St. Paul, MN 55104
(612) 645-0261   Fax—(612) 641-8969

Open to individuals experiencing age discrimination in job search. Provides job-search counseling, job leads, pension information, and retirement counseling. Call for an appointment. Sliding fee.

CENTRAL CULTURAL CHICANO INC.
2201 Nicollet Ave. So.
Minneapolis, MN 55404-3302
(612) 874-1412   Fax—(612) 874-8149

Targeted to Twin Cities Latino and Chicano communities. Job-search coaching, job leads, placement, job bank, workshops, transportation assistance, advocacy with employers. Call for appointment. Free.

CLUES
Chicanos Latinos Unidos En Servicios

2110 Nicollet Ave. So.
Minneapolis, MN 55404
(612) 871-0200

220 So. Robert St., Suite 103
St. Paul, MN 55107
(612) 292-0117

Employment assistance targeted to Hispanics. Services include career assessment, testing, job-search coaching, job bank, workshops. Broad range of social services. Call for appointment. Free.

CAREER & JOB SEARCH COUNSELING SERVICES - NON-PROFIT

■◆) EAST SIDE NEIGHBORHOOD SERVICE, INC.
❖ 1929 Second St. N.E.
Minneapolis, MN 55418
(612) 781-6011   Fax—(612) 781-9257

Open to the public. Provides career counseling, assessment, job-seeking skills training, job leads, placement services. Job placement program for low-income Hennepin County residents, ages 55 and older. Call for appointment. Free to eligible participants.

EDUCATIONAL OPPORTUNITY CENTER
Program of U.S. Department of Education

1501 Hennepin Avenue
Minneapolis, MN 55403
(612) 349-2524   Fax—(612) 341-7075

Open to adults with less than four-year college degree. Offers career planning, financial aid counseling. Helps research post-secondary schools. Call for appointment. Free.

■◆) EMPLOYMENT ACTION CENTER
❖ Lenox Community Center
6715 Minnetonka Blvd.
St. Louis Park, MN 55426
(612) 925-9195   Fax—(612) 924-1295

Open to the public. Broad-based social service organization administers government-funded and other employment programs. See separate listings for each of the programs listed below. Eligibility may be based on residency and/or income. Call for appointment. Free or low-cost.

- Minneapolis Youth Programs
- New Chance
- Pathways
- Wings North/South
- Women Achieving New Directions
- Women in Transition
- Young Dads

For an explanation of the symbols on these pages, please see pages 33-35.

ETHIOPIANS IN MINNESOTA, INC.
1821 University Ave. W., Suite 330
St. Paul, MN 55104
(612) 645-4633   Fax—(612) 645-1073

Serves Ethiopian refugees receiving public assistance, and other refugees. Offers vocational assessment, testing, job bank, job-search coaching, mentorship program, job placement, training programs. Call for appointment. Free.

■❖ EXPANDED HORIZONS
Carver-Scott Educational Cooperative
401 E. Fourth Street
Chaska, MN 55318
(612) 448-1885

Targeted to women on AFDC and others interested in training and employment. Career testing and exploration, assertiveness and self-esteem training, parenting skills. Free to eligible participants.

40 PLUS OF MINNESOTA
St. Paul, MN
(612) 683-9898

Career development and employment assistance, targeted to experienced management, technical professionals, and executives. Offers coaching by professional peers, career development programs, job bank, networking, entrepreneurial team-building. Members of affiliated associations receive additional services. Call for information.

■❖ GREATER MINNEAPOLIS CHAMBER OF COMMERCE JOBS PROGRAM
81 So. 9th St., Suite 200
Minneapolis, MN 55402
(612) 370-9188   Fax—(612) 370-9195

Targeted to low-income adults and youths. Adult program offers career and job-search counseling, educational counseling, job leads, financial assistance for day care and transportation. Free.

CAREER & JOB SEARCH COUNSELING SERVICES - NON-PROFIT

▲❖ HIRED
■◆ 1200 Plymouth Ave. No.
Minneapolis, MN 55411
(612) 529-3342

422 University Avenue
St. Paul, MN 55103
(612) 228-1118

Sabathani Center
310 E. 38th Street
Minneapolis, MN 55409
(612) 822-9071

Robbinsdale Center
4139 Regent Ave. No.
Robbinsdale, MN 55422
(612) 536-0777

Open to the public. Career and job-search counseling, resume development, coaching for networking and interviewing. Also provides resource library, training opportunities, job leads. Eligibility varies by program. Call for appointment. Free.

▲❖ HTC EMPLOYMENT AND TRAINING PROGRAMS
■◆ 7145 Harriet Ave. So.
Richfield, MN 55423
(612) 861-7481   Fax—(612) 866-2304

Employment and job-search services for residents of suburban Hennepin County. Career testing and assessment, job-seeking skills, job leads, retraining, resource library, workshops. Eligibility based on residency and income. Call for appointment. Free or low-cost.

INROADS—MPLS/ST.PAUL INC.
450 No. Syndicate, Suite 122
St. Paul, MN 55104
(612) 644-4406   Fax—(612) 649-3032

Targeted to Hispanic, Native American, and African American high school students or college freshman/sophomores who wish to pursue a four-year college degree. Applicants must meet detailed eligibility requirements. Career assessment, testing, workshops, paid internships, tutoring, job-search coaching, job leads, placement. Call for application and eligibility requirements. Free.

This chapter continues on the following page.
For an explanation of the symbols on these pages, please see pages 33-35.

JEWISH VOCATIONAL SERVICE
1500 So. Highway 100, Suite 311
Minneapolis, MN 55416
(612) 591-0300   Fax—(612) 591-0227

Open to the public. Provides job-finding strategies, career and educational counseling, assistance expanding networks, resource library, workshops. Also serves people with disabilities offering assessment, training, job placement. Flexible hourly rate.

■ JOB PLACEMENT CENTER
Carver-Scott Educational Cooperative
1138-1/2 Shakopee Town Square Mall
Shakopee, MN 55379
(612) 445-7226   Fax—(612) 368-8858

Open to the public. Offered in cooperation with Scott County Employment and Training. Job-search assistance, academic skills-building and job-seeking workshops. Call for information. Free.

LA OPORTUNIDAD
1821 University Ave. W., Suite 182
St. Paul, MN 55104
(612) 646-6115

Serves Hispanic offenders and ex-offenders. Vocational assessment, testing, job-search coaching, interviewing help, job leads, workshops, support groups. Call for appointment or drop in. Free.

❖ LAO FAMILY COMMUNITY OF MINNESOTA
976 W. Minnehaha Avenue
St. Paul, MN 55104
(612) 487-3466   Fax—(612) 487-2391

Targeted to members of Hmong community. Career assessment, job-search coaching, resume assistance, job bank, workshops. Literacy and youth employment programs. Call for appointment. Some services have eligibility requirements. Free.

CAREER & JOB SEARCH COUNSELING SERVICES - NON-PROFIT

■❖◆ LORING NICOLLET-BETHLEHEM
▶ COMMUNITY CENTER, INC.
1925 Nicollet Ave. So.
Minneapolis, MN 55403
(612) 871-2031   Fax—(612) 871-8121

Serves adults and youth. Focuses on education and training. Career assessment, job-search counseling, resume assistance, job leads. Crisis assistance. Call for an appointment. Free to eligible participants.

▲ MINNEAPOLIS AGE AND OPPORTUNITY CENTER
1801 Nicollet Ave. So.
Minneapolis, MN 55403
(612) 863-1006   Fax—(612) 863-1011

Serves Minneapolis residents, age 55 and over. Career counseling, rehirement skills workshops, free retraining opportunities, job placement. Call for appointment. Free.

▲❖■ MINNEAPOLIS URBAN LEAGUE
▶◆ 2000 Plymouth Ave. No.
Minneapolis, MN 55411
(612) 521-0342   Fax—(612) 521-8513

Open to the public but primarily serves Minneapolis residents. Assists with job-seeking/keeping skills, transportation allowance, referrals for training, job leads. Free to eligible participants.

MINNESOTA MAINSTREAM
Division of RISE, Inc.
8406 Sunset Road N.E.
Spring Lake Park, MN 55432
(612) 786-8334

Open to unemployed individuals recovering from mental illness with at least a bachelor's degree. Participants must be referred by Minnesota Division of Rehab Services. Offers complete career planning, job-search coaching, resume preparation, mentorship program, employment follow-up. Free to eligible participants.

For an explanation of the symbols on these pages, please see pages 33-35.

MINNESOTA JOB SEEKER'S SOURCEBOOK

■❖ NEW CHANCE
Program of Employment Action Center

310 E. 38th St., Suite 101
Minneapolis, MN 55409
(612) 823-5393

Targeted to AFDC recipients in Hennepin County, ages 17—22, who are high school dropouts. Vocational assessment, testing, placement, job-search assistance, training, internships. Child care provided. Free.

■◆ PHILLIPS COMMUNITY DEVELOPMENT CORP.

▶ 1014 E. Franklin Avenue
Minneapolis, MN 55404
(612) 871-2122—Job Bank
(612) 871-2435—Economic Development

Primarily serves Phillips community. Career testing, assessment, job-search assistance, vocational training, job leads. Program for entrepreneurs with grants and loans available. Free.

❖■ PILLSBURY NEIGHBORHOOD SERVICES, INC.

▶◆ Unity Center
2507 Fremont Ave. No.
Minneapolis, MN 55411
(612) 529-9267

Coyle Center
420 15th Ave. So.
Minneapolis, MN 55454
(612) 338-5282

Serves Minneapolis adults and youth. Assistance with job-readiness skills, job leads, interest and aptitude testing. Training assistance may be available. Call for appointment. Free to eligible participants.

PROJECT SELF-SUFFICIENCY
Minneapolis Public Housing Authority

600 18th Ave. No.
Minneapolis, MN 55411
(612) 342-1360   Fax—(612) 342-1367

Employment and training assistance, referrals to community resources, counseling, and advocacy. Free to eligible participants.

CAREER & JOB SEARCH COUNSELING SERVICES - NON-PROFIT

PUTTING IT ALL TOGETHER
Episcopal Community Services Inc.

373 Selby Ave., 2nd Floor
St. Paul, MN 55102
(612) 291-8553

123 No. Third St., Suite 702
Minneapolis, MN 55401
(612) 341-2680

Open to single mothers. Offers career planning, job-search counseling, workshops, on-site child care, job leads, transportation assistance, interview clothing. Call for appointment. Free.

■❖ RAMSEY COUNTY OIC
Opportunities Industrialization Center, Inc.

215 E. 9th Street
St. Paul, MN 55101
(612) 228-3285   Fax—(612) 228-3104

Targeted to unemployed and underemployed who meet poverty guidelines. Vocational testing, job-search coaching, job placement. Job club, resource library. Vocational training, GED/basic skills upgrading. Lending library of interview clothing. Sliding fee scale.

RISE, INC.

8406 Sunset Road N.E.
Spring Lake Park, MN 55432
(612) 786-8334

Targeted to individuals with disabilities. Serving seven-county metro area and Chisago County. Services include job-search coaching, training, placement, and follow-up. Also provides support services. Call for appointment. Free to eligible participants.

▶▲ ST. PAUL LABOR STUDIES

411 Main St., Room 413
St. Paul, MN 55102
(612) 290-2030   Fax—(612) 293-1989

Serves east metro residents who have lost jobs due to layoffs and plant closings. Career planning, full-service job-search counseling. Job leads, crisis assistance. Free to eligible participants.

For an explanation of the symbols on these pages, please see pages 33-35.

59

MINNESOTA JOB SEEKER'S SOURCEBOOK

▲❖▶ ST. PAUL URBAN LEAGUE
◆■ 401 Selby Avenue
St. Paul, MN 55102
(612) 224-5771   Fax—(612) 224-8009

Targeted to minority and disadvantaged individuals. Provides career planning, job-search counseling, resource library, interest/career testing, job leads. Eligibility varies by program. Free.

❖ SUBURBAN PATHWAYS
Program of Employment Action Center
6715 Minnetonka Blvd., Suite 205
St. Louis Park, MN 55426
(612) 924-1273

Open to recipients of AFDC in Hennepin County. Job-search assistance, job placement, internships, training. Self-esteem workshops, child care, transportation assistance. Free.

TAPS
Training Applicants for Placement Success
777 Raymond Avenue
St. Paul, MN 55114
(612) 646-8675   (800) 779-0777   Fax—(612) 646-1887

Open to individuals with epilepsy, ages 16 and up. Job-search coaching, resume assistance, job club, resource library, job leads, epilepsy education. Call for appointment. Free.

THE CITY, INC.
1545 E. Lake Street   1315 12th Ave. No.
Minneapolis, MN 55407   Minneapolis, MN 55411
(612) 724-3689   (612) 377-7559

Employment programs targeted to youth, adults, African-Americans, and Native Americans. Vocational assessment, testing, job-search skills, resource library, job bank, job support group. Call for appointment. Free.

CAREER & JOB SEARCH COUNSELING SERVICES - NON-PROFIT

■❖ TWIN CITIES OIC
935 Olson Memorial Highway
Minneapolis, MN 55405
(612) 377-0150   Fax—(612) 377-0156

Serves employment needs of economically disadvantaged individuals. Career assessment, testing, job-search coaching, job leads/placement. Vocational training in diverse areas. Call for appointment. Sliding fee.

UNITED CAMBODIAN ASSOCIATION OF MINNESOTA
1821 University Ave. W., Suite 325-S
St. Paul, MN 55104
(612) 645-7841   Fax—(612) 645-9334

Targeted to Cambodian community. Vocational assessment, job-search coaching, job placement, workshops, job support group. Call for appointment. Free.

VET CENTER
2480 University Avenue
St. Paul, MN 55114
(612) 644-4022   Fax—(612) 725-2234

Open to all veterans. Offers individual and group re-adjustment counseling, job-search assistance, job leads, support groups. Call for appointment or drop in. Free.

❖ WINGS
Program of Employment Action Center

3650 Fremont Ave. No.
Minneapolis, MN 55412
(612) 521-8750

430 Oak Grove, Suite B-10
Minneapolis, MN 55402
(612) 721-2714

Open to recipients of AFDC who meet residency requirements. Job-search assistance, job placement, internships, training, workshops. Child care and transportation assistance. Call for appointment. Free.

For an explanation of the symbols on these pages, please see pages 33-35.

WOMEN ACHIEVING NEW DIRECTIONS
Program of Employment Action Center

3650 Fremont Ave. No.
Minneapolis, MN 55412
(612) 521-1232   Fax—(612) 521-3818

Open to low or single-income working mothers. Job-search and job-promotion counseling, interest/aptitude testing, resource library, workshops, job leads. Call for appointment. Free or low-cost.

WOMEN IN TRANSITION
Program of Employment Action Center

6715 Minnetonka Blvd.
St. Louis Park, MN 55426
(612) 924-1261   Fax—(612) 924-1295

Targeted to women. Career planning, full-service job-search counseling, resource library, interest/career testing, job placement, self-esteem workshops. Call for appointment. Sliding fee.

❖ WOMEN'S EMPLOYMENT RESOURCE CENTER
Program of Catholic Charities

2104 Stevens Ave. So.
Minneapolis, MN 55404
(612) 872-8777

1600 University Ave., Suite 400
St. Paul, MN 55104
(612) 641-1180

Open to low-income women. Seven-week job-search preparation assistance. Career assessment, resume preparation, job application tips, interview training, mentoring opportunities, job placement. Call for appointment. Free.

WOMENVENTURE

2324 University Ave. W., Suite 200
St. Paul, MN 55114
(612) 646-3808   Fax—(612) 641-7223

Targeted to women of all ages. Many services also open to men. Career assessment/planning, individual job-search counseling, workshops, support group, and resource library. Free or sliding fee.

CAREER & JOB SEARCH COUNSELING SERVICES - NON-PROFIT

WORKING OPPORTUNITIES FOR WOMEN
2700 University W., Suite 120
St. Paul, MN 55114
(612) 647-9961   Fax—(612) 647-1424

Broad range of services includes assistance with employment goal-setting, individualized career and job-search coaching, resource library, workshops. Also provides convenient telephone counseling option. Call for appointment. Free or low-cost.

❖■ YOUNG DADS
Program of Employment Action Center
310 E. 38th St., Suite 101
Minneapolis, MN 55409
(612) 823-5393

Targeted to young fathers, ages 18—26, in Hennepin County. Provides vocational assessment, testing, job placement, job-search assistance, training, internships. Call for appointment. Free.

YOUTH EMPLOYMENT & TRAINING
Program of Blaisdell YMCA
3335 Blaisdell Ave. So.
Minneapolis, MN 55408
(612) 827-5401   Fax—(612) 827-5406

Serves employment needs of economically disadvantaged youth, ages 14—21. Assists with job-search, resume, interviewing skills, career assessment. Also offers workshops, job support group. Call for appointment. Free.

YOUTH EXPRESS
1429 Marshall Avenue
St. Paul, MN 55104
(612) 659-0613

Targeted to St. Paul youth, ages 12—17. Job-search coaching, resume and interview preparation, job leads. Call for appointment. Participant must perform community service project. Free.

For an explanation of the symbols on these pages, please see pages 33-35.

MINNESOTA JOB SEEKER'S SOURCEBOOK

NORTHERN MINNESOTA

▲❖ ARROWHEAD ECONOMIC OPPORTUNITY AGENCY
■ Open to residents of Aitkin, Carlton, Cook, Itasca, Koochiching, Lake, St. Louis Counties. Services include career assessment, testing, job-search coaching, resume and interview preparation, resource library. Job leads, retraining. Call for appointment. Fees vary.

MAIN OFFICE
702 Third Ave. So.
Virginia, MN 55792
(218) 749-2912   (800) 662-5711

AITKIN
210 Second St. N.W.
Aitkin, MN 56431
(218) 927-7046

CLOQUET
30 No. 10th Street
Cloquet, MN 55720
(218) 879-5201

DULUTH
5702 Miller Trunk Highway
Duluth, MN 55811
(218) 729-5509

ELY COMMUNITY CENTER
30 So. First Ave. East
Ely, MN 55731
(218) 365-3359

GRAND MARAIS
P.O. Box 331
Grand Marais, MN 55604
(218) 387-1134

GRAND RAPIDS
Itasca Courthouse
Grand Rapids, MN 55744
(218) 327-2830

HIBBING
c/o Stuntz Garage
1100 E. 25th Street
Hibbing, MN 55746
(218) 263-5513

INTERNATIONAL FALLS
615 4th St., Room 264
International Falls, MN 56649
(218) 283-3478

TWO HARBORS
c/o The Depot
520 South Avenue
Two Harbors, MN 55616
(218) 834-2280
(800) 223-1850

CAREER & JOB SEARCH COUNSELING SERVICES - NON-PROFIT

BEMIDJI OIC
421 Beltrami Avenue
Bemidji, MN 56601
(218) 759-2022

Targeted to Native Americans. Services include vocational assessment, testing, job-search coaching, help with resumes and interviewing, skills enhancement (GED), job placement. Drop in. Free.

FLEXWORK
Program of RESOURCE, Inc.

205 W. Second St., Suite 101
Duluth, MN 55802
(218) 722-9700

Serves individuals with disabilities referred by Minnesota Division of Rehab Services or State Services to the Blind. Career assessment, testing, job-search coaching, job leads, placement. PC skills training, paid internships. Call for information. Free to eligible participants.

▲ GREEN THUMB, INC.
Call for locations in northern Minnesota.
(800) 450-5627

Open to individuals, ages 55+ with limited income. Job training and placement in community and private sector settings. Free.

LUTHERAN SOCIAL SERVICES
Counseling Center

600 Ordean Building
424 W. Superior Street
Duluth, MN 55802
(218) 726-4769   Fax—(218) 726-1251

Open to the public. Services include career assessment, testing, individual counseling. Fees start at $90 per hour.

For an explanation of the symbols on these pages, please see pages 33-35.

■ NON-TRADITIONAL EMPLOYMENT FOR WOMEN
Northwest Private Industry Council

424 No. Broadway #A
Crookston, MN 56716
(218) 281-5180   Fax—(218) 281-5185

Targeted to women in, or seeking employment in, non-traditional fields. Offers career assessment, classroom and work training, assistance with day care and transportation. Call for appointment. Free to eligible participants.

■❖ OJIBWA EMPLOYMENT & TRAINING CENTER
White Earth Reservation Tribal Council

Box 37
Waubun, MN 56589
(218) 473-2141   (800) 726-8951

Open to Native Americans who are economically disadvantaged or AFDC recipients. Provides vocational assessment, testing, resume assistance, job leads, retraining. Classroom and on-the-job training, child care assistance. Call for appointment. Free.

PROJECT SOAR

205 W. Second Street
Duluth, MN 55812
(218) 722-3126

Targeted to displaced homemakers at all economic levels. Job and education counseling, testing, assessment, advocacy, resume development, occupation planning. Call for appointment.

CAREER & JOB SEARCH COUNSELING SERVICES - NON-PROFIT

■ RURAL MINNESOTA CEP, INC.

Open to the public but some programs have eligibility requirements. Career planning, job-search workshops, funding for post-secondary education, on-the-job training, temporary work programs. Free.

1008 Washington Ave.
P.O. Box 1690
Bemidji, MN 56601
(218) 751-8012

1919 So. 6th Street
P.O. Box 528
Brainerd, MN 56401
(218) 829-2856

803 Roosevelt Avenue
Detroit Lakes, MN 56502
(218) 847-9205

810 Fourth Ave. So.
Moorhead, MN 56560
(218) 233-1541

CENTRAL MINNESOTA

❖ EMPLOYMENT AND TRAINING CENTER
Pine Technical College
1100 Fourth Street
Pine City, MN 55063
(612) 629-6741   (800) 633-7284   Fax—(612) 629-7603

Employment assistance, free to participants of specific government funded programs. Offers career assessment, testing, job-search coaching, workshops, job leads. Call for eligibility guidelines. Free.

FLEXWORK
54 28th Ave. No.,
St. Cloud, MN 56303
(612) 259-5717

Training and job placement for disadvantaged, disabled, and sensory impaired individuals re-entering the workforce. Must be referred by the Division of Rehabilitation Services or State Services for the Blind. Free to eligible individuals.

For an explanation of the symbols on these pages, please see pages 33-35.

FUNCTIONAL INDUSTRIES, INC.
Sher-Wright Employment Program
1801 Highway 25
Buffalo, MN 55313
(612) 682-4336   Fax—(612) 338-3097 *4

Open only to residents of Sherburne and Wright Counties with serious and persistent mental illness. Provides job placement, resume preparation, job leads. Call for appointment. Free.

▲ GREEN THUMB, INC.
(800) 450-5627
219 So. Jefferson
Wadena, MN 56482
(218) 631-3483   Fax—(218) 631-3077

Open to individuals, ages 55 and up, with limited incomes. On-site job training and placement in community and private sector settings. Call for locations in central Minnesota. Free.

MIDWEST FARMWORKER EMPLOYMENT & TRAINING, INC.
P.O. Box 1231
St. Cloud, MN 56302-1231
(612) 253-7010

Targeted to migrant, seasonal farm or ranch workers seeking full-time permanent employment. Training, on-the-job training, job-search coaching, and placement. Call for information. Free.

OPPORTUNITY TRAINING CENTER, INC.
318 14th Ave. No.
St. Cloud, MN 56302
(612) 252-2651

For persons with emotional, developmental and/or physical disabilities referred by Division of Rehabilitation Services, Veteran's Administration or rehabilitation counselor. Offers vocational evaluation, training, and job placement assistance. Call for information and fees.

CAREER & JOB SEARCH COUNSELING SERVICES - NON-PROFIT

❖■ PRIVATE INDUSTRY COUNCIL 5
▶◆ 500 Elm St. East
P.O. Box 579
Annandale, MN 55302
(612) 274-2650   (800) 284-7425   Fax—(612) 274-3516

Employment assistance, free to eligible participants of government funded programs. Provides career assessment, testing, resume preparation, job leads, job bank, workshops. Call for appointment.

RURAL EMPLOYMENT PLACEMENT PROJECT
Wacosa

620 Sundial Drive
Waite Park, MN 56387
(612) 251-0087   Fax—(612) 259-4679

Open to individuals with severe disabilities. Offers career assessment, job-search coaching, job placement, resource library. Call for appointment. Sliding fee.

STEPPING STONES
Heartland Community Action

310 So. First Street
Box 1359
Willmar, MN 56201
(612) 235-0850   Fax—(612) 235-7703

Targeted to divorced or separated individuals who have lost their means of support. Services include career assessment, testing, resume preparation, job-search coaching, resource library. Call for appointment. Sliding fee. Free to low-income.

This chapter continues on the following page.
For an explanation of the symbols on these pages, please see pages 33-35.

■ RURAL MINNESOTA CEP, INC.

118 So. Mill St., Suite 302
P.O. Box 161
Fergus Falls, MN 56537
(218) 736-6963

202 No. Fourth Street
P.O. Box 97
Staples, MN 56479
(218) 894-3771

211 First St. S.E.
P.O. Box 332
Little Falls, MN 56345
(612) 632-2356

Open to the public but certain programs have eligibility requirements. Offers career planning, job-search workshops, funding for post-secondary education, on-the-job training, temporary work programs. Drop in or call. Free to eligible participants.

WINGS

700 W. Germain Street
St. Cloud, MN 56301
(612) 251-1612

Open to women who have lost their means of support. Services provided through 12-week workshops. Weekly training in self-confidence, esteem building, interviewing skills, resume development. Call for appointment. Free to eligible participants.

SOUTHERN MINNESOTA

■ CHOICES — S.E. MINNESOTA

851 30th Ave. S.E.
Rochester, MN 55904
(507) 280-5510   (800) 657-3716

Targeted to displaced homemakers. Career assessment, testing, workshops, job leads, resource library, job-search coaching. Support groups, and financial workshops. Call for appointment. Free to eligible participants.

CAREER & JOB SEARCH COUNSELING SERVICES - NON-PROFIT

▲ GREEN THUMB, INC.
Call for locations in southern Minnesota.
(800) 450-5627

Open to individuals, age 55 and up, with limited income. On-site job training and placement in community and private sector settings. Free.

■ ▶ LIFE-WORK PLANNING CENTER
Nichols Center, 410 Jackson
Mankato, MN 56001
(507) 345-1577

Targeted to women in transition. Offers career assessment, testing, workshops, job-search coaching, resource library, job leads. Hands-on computer access, support groups, services for displaced homemakers, entrepreneurial groups. Culturally sensitive, bilingual (Spanish-English). Call for appointment. Free to eligible participants.

■ MAINSTAY, INC.
308 No. Third Street
Marshall, MN 56258
(800) 554-2481   (507) 537-1546   Fax—(507) 537-4550

Targeted to displaced homemakers in southwestern Minnesota. Provides vocational assessment, testing, job-search coaching, workshops, job placement, resource library. Workshops for mentally ill women in community residences. Call for appointment. Sliding fee.

▲❖ MINNESOTA VALLEY ACTION COUNCIL, INC.
■ Family Services Department
P.O. Box 3327
410 Jackson Street
Mankato, MN 56002
(507) 345-6822   (800) 767-7139

Targeted to economically disadvantaged individuals. Vocational assessment, testing, job leads, workshops, training for GED. Call for appointment. Free to eligible participants.

For an explanation of the symbols on these pages, please see pages 33-35.

❖ OLMSTED COMMUNITY ACTION PROGRAM

1421 Third Ave. S.E.
Rochester, MN 55904
(507) 285-8785   Fax—(507) 285-8401

Employment assistance, free to eligible participants. Career assessment, testing, job-search coaching, job leads, job club, workshops. Call for information about eligibility requirements.

◆❖ PRIVATE INDUSTRY COUNCIL—AUSTIN
Career Planning and Placement

1900 8th Ave. N.W.
Austin, MN 55912
(507) 433-0685   Fax—(507) 433-0665

Employment assistance, free to low-income participants. Career assessment, testing, job-search coaching, workshops, job placement, resource library, job club. Call for appointment.

❖■ S.E. MINNESOTA JOB TRAINING CENTER
▶◆ 300 11th Ave. N.W.
Rochester, MN 55901
(507) 252-2463   (800) 543-5627   Fax—(507) 252-2495

Targeted to disadvantaged and low-income individuals. Career assessment, testing, job-search coaching, resume and interview preparation. Workshops, classes, internships, job leads, and retraining. Call for appointment or drop in. Free.

❖■ S.E. MINNESOTA
▶◆ PRIVATE INDUSTRY COUNCIL, INC.

300 11th Ave. N.W., Suite 110
Rochester, MN 55901
(507) 252-2442   Fax—(507) 252-2495

Targeted to disadvantaged and low-income individuals. Career assessment, testing, job-search coaching, job leads. Computer and life skills training. Math and English updating. Drop in. Free.

CAREER & JOB SEARCH COUNSELING SERVICES - NON-PROFIT

❖▲❱ S.W. MINNESOTA
■◆ PRIVATE INDUSTRY COUNCIL
Call for locations in Marshall, Worthington, Montevideo.
1424 E. College Drive
P.O. Box 3097
Marshall, MN 56258
(507) 532-4411   (800) 422-0687   Fax—(507) 532-4703

Employment assistance, free to eligible participants of government funded programs. Career assessment, job-search coaching, job leads. On-the-job and classroom training. Relocation, day care and transportation assistance. Call for appointment.

YOUTH EMPLOYMENT PROJECT, INC.
208 City Hall
Rochester, MN 55902
(507) 287-2345

Open to youth, ages 13—19. Employment clearinghouse which matches youth to jobs in child care, moving, and yard work. Call for appointment and fees.

WESTERN WISCONSIN

TURNAROUND
304 No. Sixth Street
La Crosse, WI 54602
(608) 785-9436

770 Scheidler Road
Chippewa Falls, WI 54729
(715) 723-0261

920 River Heights Road
Menomonie, WI 54751
(715) 235-7631

620 W. Clairemont Avenue
Eau Claire, WI 54701
(715) 833-6257

Employment assistance targeted to eligible displaced homemakers. Services include career assessment, testing, job-search coaching, and job leads. Call for appointment. Free.

For an explanation of the symbols on these pages, please see pages 33-35.

■ WEST CENTRAL WISCONSIN PRIVATE INDUSTRY COUNCIL
Vocational Assessment Workshop

2105 Stout Road
Menomonie, WI 54751
(715) 232-1412   (800) 472-5522 (WI only)

Employment assistance, free to eligible participants of government funded programs. Serving Barron, Chippewa, Clark, Dunn, Eau Claire, Pepin, Pierce, Polk, St. Croix Counties. Career assessment, testing, job-search coaching, resume preparation, job leads, on-the-job training, GED preparation, workshops, job bulletins. Drop in.

▲ WISCONSIN GREEN THUMB, INC.

Call or write for locations in 56 Wisconsin counties

204 Clark County Courthouse
Neillsville, WI 54456
(715) 743-4636

Open to individuals, ages 55 and up, with limited income. Serving Eau Claire County. On-site job training and placement in community and private sector settings. Free.

CAREER & JOB SEARCH COUNSELING SERVICES

Private Sector

In this section you will find career and job search counseling services offered by the private sector. It's not surprising to encounter experts in this area who help senior-level management and other professionals deal with job transition.

For some folks, private sector resources make good sense. Although often—but not always—pricier than non-profits, the business-like environment and wide selection of services may be appropriate and familiar to some corporate types. Larger firms may offer amenities like telephone answering services, office space, and secretarial assistance.

But these extras do not come cheap. Some career and job-search counseling services charge $2,500 or more for a full-service job counseling package. On the other hand, some one-person shops and smaller firms staffed by licensed psychologists or career counselors may charge by the hour or project, at a much less expensive scale.

The consideration of fees is especially important in this section where the cost can be potentially so high. Before you make any financial commitments, research the company thoroughly. Ask for references and credentials. Be certain that you understand what you will receive for your money. What kind of testing is used? What will it measure and show? What will you gain from this service?

There are many experienced career professionals in this community, but at the present time in Minnesota, there is no competency-based system for licensing professional career counselors. That means that, theoretically, anyone can enter into the business of "career consulting" without first having attained a minimum level of education or training. For this reason, it's wise to be a careful and intelligent consumer.

TWIN CITIES

ALL-PROFESSIONAL CAREER MANAGEMENT
1550 E. 79th St., Suite 680
Bloomington, MN 55425
(612) 854-7705

Services include career planning, testing, individualized and group counseling. Emphasis on interview preparation. Provides resource library, support groups. Call for appointment. Fees vary by project.

ALLEN AND ASSOCIATES
6600 France Ave. So.
Edina, MN 55435
(612) 925-9646

Offers job-search coaching, career assessment, resume preparation, marketing letters, and database of employers. Also provides mailing and answering services, office space, resource library, reference checking. Call for information and fees.

CAREER & JOB SEARCH COUNSELING - PRIVATE SECTOR

APPLE VALLEY COUNSELING CLINIC
7373 147th St., Suite 196
Apple Valley, MN 55124
(612) 431-6228

Licensed psychologist provides career assessment, testing, job-search coaching, resume assistance, job leads, and workshops. Call for appointment. Hourly fees start at $80.

ASSOCIATED CAREER SERVICES, INC.
1611 W. County Road B, Suite 120
Roseville, MN 55113
(612) 631-9115

Services include career planning, assessment, resume development. Also provides resource library, computerized career exploration. Fees are hourly, or based on services required. Call for appointment.

BERNARD HALDANE ASSOCIATES
3433 Broadway St. N.E., Suite 440
Minneapolis, MN 55413
(612) 378-0600

Specializes in working with management and professional personnel, entry through senior level. Provides career assessment and assistance with professional job marketing. Call for appointment and fees.

BILEK CONSULTING
4620 W. 77th St., Suite 160
Edina, MN 55435
(612) 832-0557

Services include coaching in strategic market positioning, career assessment, testing, job-search skills. Also offers workshops and resource library. Call for appointment and fees.

This chapter continues on the following page.

CAREER DYNAMICS, INC.
8400 Normandale Lake Blvd., Suite 1220
Bloomington, MN 55437
(612) 921-2378

Services include assistance with career goal-setting and job-search strategy, resume preparation, and cold-calling skills. Also provides job leads and office space by special arrangement. Call for appointment and fees.

CENTER FOR COUNSELING AND STRESS MANAGEMENT
1204 Harmon Place
Minneapolis, MN 55403
(612) 333-1766

Provides career development assistance by licensed psychologist including testing, assessment, career decision-making, and job-search strategies. Call for appointment. Sliding fee scale.

CRAIG GROUP INTERNATIONAL
Highway 169 and Anderson Lakes Parkway
Eden Prairie, MN 55344-3910
(612) 944-1759

Specializes in assisting with career change. Services include individual/group career consulting, assistance with goal-setting, job-search strategy, help in utilizing the hidden job market, video-taped interview coaching. Call for appointment and fees.

DAVID D. CADY AND ASSOCIATES
1660 S. Highway 100, Suite 122
St. Louis Park, MN 55416
(612) 690-2755

Targeted to professional and technical personnel. Provides career assessment, testing, resume preparation, assistance with interviewing and salary negotiations. Job club, resource library, workshops. Call for appointment and fees.

CAREER & JOB SEARCH COUNSELING - PRIVATE SECTOR

DEVELOPMENTAL RESOURCES, INC.
100 Portland Ave., Suite 225
Minneapolis, MN 55401
(612) 341-2250

Organizational and career psychologists/consultants provide career testing, marketing, and job-search support to individuals and organizations. Call for information and fees.

DOUGLAS ASSOCIATES
Darnel Road and Anderson Lakes Parkway
Eden Prairie, MN 55347
(612) 946-1810

Targeted to professionals, middle-management and above. Career assessment, testing, job-search coaching, resume/interview assistance, job leads, workshops. Call for appointment. Hourly fees start at $75. Package services available.

GARY JOHNSON & ASSOCIATES
Licensed Psychologist/Futurist
995 Wildwood Road
St. Paul, MN 55115
(612) 770-0666

Provides career consultation and assistance exploring work and career options in the new economy. Also provides career testing. Fees vary depending on services selected. Call for appointment.

INTELACTION INC., CAREER SERVICES
4930 W. 77th St., Suite 237
Edina, MN 55435
(612) 893-9692

Services include background assessment, career planning, testing, letter/resume writing, assistance with interviewing, negotiation, and networking skills. Provides office space, resource library. Fees vary by project. Call for appointment.

This chapter continues on the following page.

KURENITZ & ASSOCIATES
205 Willow Creek Plaza
9800 Shelard Parkway
Plymouth, MN 55441
(612) 595-4434

Assists in career/life planning and job transition services such as goal-setting, interviewing assistance, resume construction, job-search strategies. Fees are hourly on project basis. Call for appointment. Free initial consultation.

L.D.A. ENTERPRISES
P.O. Box 201355
Bloomington, MN 55420
(612) 835-0927

Assists with employment goal-setting, personal marketing, resume development, networking, interviewing, negotiating. Offers resource library, job leads, on-going support. Call for appointment and fees.

LIFE DIMENSIONS, INC.
3060 Magnolia No.
Minneapolis, MN 55441-2858
(612) 559-1177

Offers job-search coaching, career assessment, testing, resume and interview assistance, career/life management groups, workshops. Facilitates national network of career and life management consultants. Call for appointment and fees.

LOFTUS BROWN-WESCOTT, INC.
Kickernick Bldg., Suite 790
430 First Ave. No.
Minneapolis, MN 55401
(612) 341-1024

Provides assistance with employment goal-setting and strategy, industry and job research skills. Call for appointment. Fees vary by services required.

CAREER & JOB SEARCH COUNSELING - PRIVATE SECTOR

MARKET SHARE INC.
155 Fifth Ave. So., Suite 350
Minneapolis, MN 55401
(612) 375-9277

Coaching in employment goal-setting and career assessment, marketing strategies, employer contact research, entrepreneurial and business planning. Assists in preparation of resumes/cover letters. Resource library available. Call for appointment and fees.

MINNESOTA HUMAN DEVELOPMENT CONSULTANTS, INC.
1409 Willow St., Suite 400
Minneapolis, MN 55403
(612) 870-1242

Services provided by licensed consulting psychologists, include vocational testing, career and professional development. Call for appointment. Fees are hourly or on a project basis.

OUTPLACEMENT INTERNATIONAL MINNESOTA
5821 Cedar Lake Road
Minneapolis, MN 55416
(612) 525-1475

Offers career assessment, testing, job-search coaching, resume and interview preparation. Workshops, job leads, retraining. Specializes in outplacement services. Call for appointment and fees.

PATHFINDER PERSONNEL SERVICES, INC.
708 No. First St., Suite 244
Minneapolis, MN 55401
(612) 333-5944

Provides a variety of assessment tests, guided exploration of job opportunities, and employment alternatives. Resume/letter-writing assistance, interview and telephone contact training, networking, job leads. Call for appointment. Hourly and package fees.

This chapter continues on the following page.

PERSONNEL DECISIONS, INCORPORATED (PDI)
7760 France Ave. So., Suite 750
Minneapolis, MN 55435
(612) 921-0400

Career transition services include employment goal-setting and strategizing, resume development, personal marketing. Also provides office space, secretarial services, resource library, support group, job leads. Call for appointment and fees.

PROFESSIONAL CAREER ALTERNATIVES
430 First Ave. No., Suite 630
Minneapolis, MN 55401
(612) 340-9544

Targeted to attorneys and professionals. Career assessment and testing, job-search and career advancement coaching, resume preparation, workshops. Call for appointment and fees.

PROTOTYPE CAREER SERVICES
626 Armstrong Avenue
St. Paul, MN 55102
(612) 224-2856   (800) 368-3197

Targeted to workers who have lost jobs due to layoffs. One-to-one consulting, job-search workshops, resume assistance, videotaped interview coaching. Employer/career research. Evening/weekend appointments. Hourly fees. Two Twin Cities locations.

RESOURCE PUBLISHING GROUP INC.
10709 Wayzata Blvd., Suite 250
Minnetonka, MN 55305
(612) 545-5980   Fax—(612) 545-9241

Publisher of a broad range of career and job-search publications including the Minnesota Job Seeker's Sourcebook, Twin Cities Job Seeker's Calendar, and a publication series designed for employers to provide to employees in transition for outplacement or internal transition needs. Individualized and group counseling services also available. Call for information.

CAREER & JOB SEARCH COUNSELING - PRIVATE SECTOR

RICHARD E. ANDREA, PH.D
Licensed Consulting Psychologist
Nationally Certified Career Counselor

1399 Geneva Ave. Suite 202
Oakdale, MN 55128
(612) 738-6600

Provides career counseling and testing, job-seeking skills training, and personal counseling for job-related conflicts. Career resource library on occupational information and school programs. Call for appointment. Hourly or package fees.

SORENSEN & ASSOCIATES, INC.

7600 France Ave. So., Suite 101
Edina, MN 55435
(612) 831-3516

Job transition and career advancement service identifies individual's interests, values, and talents and matches them to over 60,000 career options to find ideal niche. Call for appointment and fees.

STEFFEN CAREER SERVICES, INC.

Burnsville, MN 55337
(612) 891-6033

Provides career assessment and testing, assistance with interviewing, salary negotiations, and marketplace evaluation. Call for appointment and fees.

THE ARTHUR GROUP

10125 Crosstown Circle, Suite 300
Eden Prairie, MN 55344
(612) 941-1116

Assistance with employment goal-setting and strategy, personal marketing, resume development, job-search skills. Resource library, job leads, on-going support. Call for appointment and fees.

This chapter continues on the following page.

THE CAREER BRIDGE, INC.
2665 Long Lake Road, Suite 220
Roseville, MN 55113
(612) 631-3015

Services include self-evaluation and personal counseling for career change due to injury. Call for appointment. Hourly and package fees. Injury cases may be covered by insurance.

THE MEREDITH COMPANY OF MINNESOTA
5001 W. 80th St., Suite 500
Minneapolis, MN 55437
(612) 830-0946

Career management services include assessment and goal-setting, interview training, network building, job transition techniques, retirement planning. Call for appointment and fees.

WORK/LIFE TRANSITIONS
620 Mendelssohn Ave. No., Suite 168
Golden Valley, MN 55427
(612) 544-4580

Services include assistance in career assessment, employment goal-setting and strategy, resume development, expert coaching to improve networking, interviewing, and negotiating skills. Offers resource library, on-going support. Call for appointment. Hourly rate.

WORKING OPTIONS
Division of Vocational Rehabilitation Associates
333 Washington Ave. No., Suite 202
Minneapolis, MN 55401
(612) 349-9865

Offers vocational testing, career planning, resume preparation, job-seeking instruction. Access to occupational and educational resource information. Call for appointment. Hourly and package fees.

CAREER & JOB SEARCH COUNSELING - PRIVATE SECTOR

NORTHERN MINNESOTA

GINSBERG PSYCHOLOGICAL SERVICE
210 W. Superior Street
Duluth, MN 55802
(218) 726-0509

Services include career assessment, testing, job-search coaching, workshops. Call for appointment. Hourly fees start at $80.

CENTRAL MINNESOTA

COMPLETE CAREER SERVICES
325 33rd Ave. No.
St. Cloud, MN 56303
(612) 255-0685

Provides job placement to injured workers and career services to the public. Offers resume-writing assistance, testing, and job-search counseling. Call for appointment. Hourly fees start at $50.

DONOVAN & ASSOCIATES
1002 W. Fourth Street
Morris, MN 56267
(612) 589-6065

Nationally certified career counselor provides career assessment, testing, job-search coaching, workshops, and job placement. Call for appointment. Sliding fee scale.

PROCESSUS
600 25th Ave. So., Suite 210
St. Cloud, MN 56301
(612) 252-2976

Consulting psychologist helps individuals plan career change. Offers testing, one-to-one counseling, men's support groups. Call for appointment and fees. Free initial consultation.

SOUTHERN MINNESOTA

LIFE DEVELOPMENT COUNSELING
Crossroad House
331 Dillon Avenue
Mankato, MN 56001
(507) 625-6862

Specializes in life and career planning. Provides career assessment, testing, job-search coaching, and workshops. Sliding fee.

ROCHESTER CAREER COUNSELING CENTER
Rochester, MN 55904
(507) 288-3890

Nationally certified career counselor offers career assessment and testing, job-search coaching. Also provides job leads and workshops. Call for appointment and fees.

WESTERN WISCONSIN

BRIARWOOD CONSULTANTS
2713 Patton Street
Eau Claire, WI 54701
(715) 834-2200

Services include career counseling, resume services, assistance with job-search procedures, interviewing and salary negotiations. Call for appointment. Fees vary by services required.

THE PRACTICE OF KINLEIN
1507 Tower Ave., Suite 419
Superior, WI 54880
(715) 394-6291

Offers career exploration and counseling, and general assistance for direction in living. Call for appointment. Sliding fee.

Resume Preparation Services

Probably no single component of the job hunting process gets more press and attention than the resume. And no wonder. Right or wrong, some experts say that jobs can be had—or lost—with this one document.

That's why so many job seekers turn to resume specialists. A good resume preparer can help you articulate your experience, responsibilities and skills, and sum it up in a page or two which honestly represents your employment profile.

But judging who's a "good resume preparer" can be a tricky business.

Certainly you may be "good" enough to write your own resume, especially if you're a clear thinker with a firm grasp on your career experience. Or you can turn to Cousin Norm who wrote a "great" resume—and look at the job he just got. Most career and job-search counseling services, found in the previous sections, list resume development prominently in their palette of qualified job hunting support services.

Job hunters have yet another good option: Choosing from among the scores of resume preparation businesses. Don't look for career counseling or job hunting advice at these specialized services. Resumes and related materials are generally their only business.

Expect to find a tremendous variation of qualifications, services, and fees among resume preparers. Some services are staffed by professional writers. Others are provided by home-based secretarial businesses. One preparer may write your resume after an extensive interview, leaving the printing to you or an outside service. Others handle production and printing—no writing provided. Some shops do it all.

If you elect to use a resume preparation service, call several and screen them by phone. Visit a few, and carefully interview the preparer. Ask about fees (many offer package prices, others charge by the hour). Insist on seeing a portfolio of samples. Check out their writing style, design selection, paper stock, and printing quality.

Determine whether the service has produced resumes for comparable jobs in your field. If you're a senior systems analyst, for example, think twice before you contract with a service that typically prepares resumes for entry-level clerical workers.

Fees usually start at $25. For that, a service will probably begin with your hand-written resume, key it into a computer and hand over a master page that you can have printed or photocopied elsewhere. Resume packages generally include consultation, writing, production, and delivery of the final product. Packages can start at $50 and range upwards to $200 or more.

Remember: A well-written resume doesn't necessarily get you the job, but a poorly written resume could lessen your chances. Do some street-wise research. Determine the degree of resume sophistication in your industry. Examine your budget and needs, and proceed accordingly. You may need more than resume assistance. If so, seek out a full-service career and job-search specialist.

RESUME PREPARATION SERVICES

TWIN CITIES

A PLUS TYPING AND WORD PROCESSING
Champlin, MN 55316
(612) 427-1025   Fax—(612) 323-9574

Services include client interviews, resume writing, layout, cover letters, laser printing, disk storage. Laser-printed resumes start at $25. Call for appointment.

ABILITY RESUME SERVICES
1111 W. 22nd St., Suite 109
Minneapolis, MN 55405
(612) 377-6939

Services include client consultation, resume writing, editing, layout, cover letters, and reference sheets. Disk storage. Fees vary by services required. Call for appointment.

BUSINESS OFFICE SUPPORT SERVICES
2499 Rice St., Suite 240
St. Paul, MN 55113
(612) 490-0172

Client consultation, resume writing and editing, disk storage. Laser printouts available. Fees start at $30 for desktop publishing of a one-page resume. Additional charge for consultation. Call for information.

CORPORATE INFORMATION TECHNOLOGY SERVICES
St. Paul, MN 55104
(612) 646-2476

Free initial visit. Provides resume writing, editing, layout, formatting. Cover letters, job-search mailings. Laser printouts, disk storage. Call for appointment. Fees start at $20 per page.

This chapter continues on the following page.

FINE LINE RESUME SERVICE
3030 Harbor Lane, Suite 125
Plymouth, MN 55447
(612) 553-9937   Fax—(612) 553-0077

Free initial consultation. Services include resume writing, editing, layout, cover letters, laser printing, disk storage. Resume-writing fees start at $75. Call for appointment.

FITZGERALD RESUME WRITING AND CAREER COUNSELING
Eagan, MN 55122
(612) 452-5536

Free initial visit. Services include resume writing, editing, layout, cover-letter writing, laser printing, and disk storage. Also conducts industry research, charged by the hour. Fees start at $12. Call for an appointment.

GISLESON WRITING SERVICES
St. Paul, MN 55108
(612) 644-6408   Fax—(612) 645-3530

Services include resume writing, editing, layout, laser printing (600 dpi laser printer). Cover letters, disk storage, applications, and SF 171's. Fees start at $25 for typesetting and printing of a one-page resume. Hourly fees, $50. Call for an appointment. Weekday, weekend, and evening appointments available.

INFORMATION MANAGEMENT SYSTEMS, INC.
2200 University Ave. W., Suite 130
St. Paul, MN 55114
(612) 642-2525   Fax—(612) 642-2520

Offers consultation, profile development and writing, printing, letters, and support materials. Disk access and storage. Fees reflect services required. Call for appointment.

RESUME PREPARATION SERVICES

KATHLEEN BROGAN
Richfield, MN 55423
(612) 866-8940   Fax—(612) 869-2927

Offers writing, editing, layout, and formatting of resumes and job-search correspondence. Laser printouts and disk storage available. Free initial visit. Fees start at $35. Call for appointment.

L & S OFFICE SERVICES
St. Paul, MN 55105
(612) 690-1213

Entry-level to mid-management resumes. Services include resume writing, layout, laser printing, cover letters, disk storage, photocopies. Fees start at $25 per hour. Call for appointment.

OMNI/OFFICEPLUS
8400 Normandale Lake Blvd.
Bloomington, MN 55437
(612) 921-2300

601 Lakeshore Pkwy.
Minnetonka, MN 55343
(612) 449-5100

Services include resume writing/editing, layout, cover letters, laser printing, disk storage. Fees start at $25 for computer-generated, laser-printed one-page resume. Call for appointment.

PENCRAFT RESUME SERVICE
1020 E. 146th St., Suite 141-E
Burnsville, MN 55337
(612) 431-5962

Services include resume writing, editing, layout, cover letters, laser printing, disk storage. Computer-generated, laser-printed resumes start at $30. Package prices. Call for appointment.

PERSONAL PROFILE SERVICES
Falcon Heights, MN 55108
(612) 646-9636

Conducts in-depth, taped interview, and provides resume and other writing. Directed resumes and cover letters start at $75. Disk storage. Call for appointment.

PERSPECTIVES MEDIA COMMUNICATIONS
Stillwater, MN 55082
(612) 436-2025

Offers client consultation, resume writing and layout, cover letters, laser printouts, disk storage. Call for appointment and fees.

PROFESSIONAL PROFILES
Lakeville, MN 55044
(612) 435-1952   Fax—(612) 898-1576

Services include client consultation, resume writing, layout, formatting, laser printouts. Cover letters, disk storage. Free initial visit. Call for appointment. Affordable resume packages.

RESUME SPECIALISTS
3033 Excelsior Blvd., Suite 444
Minneapolis, MN 55416
(612) 928-0660

Resume writing, layout, cover letters, laser printing, job-search coaching, and interview preparation. Call for appointment and fees.

STANDBY SECRETARIES, INC.
2233 Hamline Ave., Suite 511
Roseville, MN 55113
(612) 636-2788

Resume writing, layout, cover letters, laser printing, disk storage. Fees start at $25 for word processed, two-page resume with laser printout.

SUPERIOR CAREER PROFESSIONALS
9336 Washburn Ave. North
Brooklyn Park, MN 55444
(612) 493-5684

One Appletree Square
Bloomington, MN 55425
(612) 493-5684

Client consultation, resume writing, layout and laser printing. Also prepares cover letters, offers job-search consulting, and disk storage. Fees start at $85 for full-service preparation. Call for appointment.

RESUME PREPARATION SERVICES

THE RESUME PLACE
Plymouth, MN
(612) 559-4204   Fax—(612) 551-1932

Consultation, resume writing/editing, layout, cover letters, laser printing, disk storage. Full-service resume package starts at $150.

THE RESUME SHOP
Stillwater, MN 55082
(612) 439-6903

Free initial consultation. Resume writing, layout, formatting, printouts. Cover letters, disk storage. Business portfolios, business cards and brochures. Hourly fees start at $20. Call for appointment.

NORTHERN MINNESOTA

DIANE'S SECRETARIAL SERVICE
102 First Street N.W.
Bemidji, MN 56601
(218) 751-7408   Fax—(218) 751-2141

Provides resume writing, typing, formatting, printouts, cover letters, disk storage. Resume typing starts at $12. Other services offered at additional cost. Call for appointment.

LINDA'S PAGEWORKS
Duluth, MN 55811
(218) 729-7656—Phone/Fax

Services include resume and cover-letter writing, typing, formatting, and printouts. Also provides disk storage; secretarial and desktop publishing services. Basic package starts at $15. Call for appointment.

This chapter continues on the following page.

MAY WE HELP II
500 Folz Blvd.
P.O. Box 310
Moose Lake, MN 55767
(218) 485-4123—Phone/Fax

Free initial visit. Resume writing, editing, formatting, printouts. Job applications, cover letters, disk storage. Also helps clients track job leads at no charge. Resumes start at $20. Call for appointment.

NORTHLAND BUSINESS SERVICES
Bemidji, MN 56601
(218) 759-1689

Free initial visit. Resume writing and formatting, cover letters, reference sheets, job-search correspondence. Laser printouts, disk storage for one year. Suite rentals, secretarial services. Call for appointment. Resumes start at $10.

SECRETARY ON CALL
Duluth, MN 55812
(218) 724-6484—Phone/Fax

Specializes in resumes for sales, management, and professionals. Services include client consultation, resume writing, editing, formatting, cover letters, laser printouts, disk storage. Free initial visit. Packages start at $40. Call for appointment.

VIDEO UNLIMITED
301 W. First St., Suite 303
Duluth, MN 55802
(218) 722-8820

Videotaped resumes feature clients discussing job experience, achievements, goals, etc. for prospective employers. Basic package, $75, with one video. Hourly fees: $35. Call for appointment.

RESUME PREPARATION SERVICES

WORD PROCESSING OF DULUTH
394 Lake Ave. So., Suite 303
Duluth, MN 55802
(218) 722-6911   Fax—(218) 722-0506

Provides client consultation, resume writing, editing, layout, formatting, laser printouts, disk storage. Assistance with writing, editing and typing cover letters and other job-search correspondence. Prepares reference page, salary history charts. Also offers general secretarial services. Basic package starts at $21. Call for appointment.

CENTRAL MINNESOTA

ADMINISTRATIVE OFFICE SERVICES, INC.
400 E. St. Germain
St. Cloud, MN 56304
(612) 253-2532

Fees start at $20 for one-page resume. Guarantees delivery in 24 hours. After-hours and weekend services by appointment.

CITY SECRETARY INC.
916 Broadway
Alexandria, MN 56308
(612) 763-5881

Resume writing, formatting, cover letters, laser printouts, disk storage. Copying/answering services, mailings, send/receive faxes. Call for appointment. Resume packages start at $24.50.

ELECTRONIC INK
St. Cloud, MN 56301
(612) 253-0975.

Client consultation, resume writing, editing and layout. Also provides cover letters, laser printing, disk storage. Call for appointment. Fees start at $75 for resume development and production.

This chapter continues on the following page.

EMPLOYMENT PLUS
920 W. Litchfield Avenue
Willmar, MN 56201
(612) 235-1707   Fax—(612) 235-8510

Resume writing, formatting, cover letters, laser printouts, disk storage. Basic resume package starts at $35. Call for appointment.

EXECUTIVE SUITES ON FIRST
2015 First St. So.
Willmar, MN 56201
(612) 235-9512   Fax—(612) 235-8633

Free initial visit. Resume writing, formatting, cover letters, laser printouts, disk storage. Call for information and fees.

KINKO'S COPY CENTER
211 Fifth Ave. So.
St. Cloud, MN 56301
(612) 259-1224

Free instruction on Macintosh computers to write and format resumes and cover letters. Kinko's also can format and print resumes.

L-J ENTERPRISES
Hutchinson, MN 55350
(612) 587-7318

Free initial consultation. Resume writing, layout, formatting, printouts. Cover letters, disk storage. Mass mailings and secretarial services. Call for information and fees.

PROFESSIONAL TYPING
St. Cloud, MN 56303
(612) 251-2741

Fees start at $20 to type and format a one-page resume. Updates are available at half-cost for the first year. Also offers typing service for cover letters and job-search correspondence.

RESUME PREPARATION SERVICES

THE SECRETARIAN
116 Main St. South
Hutchinson, MN 55350
(612) 587-7002   Fax—(612) 587-7822

Free initial visit. Resume writing, layout, formatting, printouts. Cover letters, disk storage. Resumes start at $15. Call for appointment.

WML
11 First Ave. So.
Buffalo, MN 55313
(612) 682-5906   Fax—(612) 682-4791

Free initial consultation. Services include resume writing, layout and formatting, printouts. Also provides cover letters and disk storage. Starting prices for resume packages range from $15-30.

SOUTHERN MINNESOTA

CAREER CONNECTIONS
P.O. Box 266
Albert Lea, MN 56007
(507) 373-1736

Free initial consultation. Resume writing, layout, formatting, printouts. Cover letters, disk storage. Provides resume reference manual with initial deposit. Prices start at $45. Call for appointment.

DESIGN RESUME & PAGE LAYOUT
Rochester, MN 55902
(507) 285-1657   Fax—(507) 252-8072

Client consultation, resume writing, layout, formatting, laser printouts. Cover letters, disk storage, wallet-size networking cards. Free initial visit. Prices start at $25. Call for appointment.

This chapter continues on the following page.

MIDTOWN SECRETARIAL SERVICES

Armory Center
217 Plum St., Suite 150
Red Wing, MN 55066
(612) 388-2261   (800) 829-5354

427 Vermillion Street
Hastings, MN 55033
(612) 438-3734

Free initial consultation. Resume writing, layout, formatting, printouts. Cover letters, disk storage. Resume packages start at $25. Call for appointment.

PERSONAL TOUCH OFFICE SERVICES

403 Division Street
Northfield, MN 55057
(507) 645-8811   Fax—(507) 645-9291

Client consultation, resume writing, layout, formatting, laser printouts. Cover letters, disk storage. Free initial visit. Call for appointment. Fees vary by services required.

PETERSON TYPING SERVICE

Rochester, MN 55902
(507) 285-1350

Consultation interview, resume writing, editing, typing. Cover letters, laser printing, disk storage. Free first visit. Resume packages start at $35. Call for appointment.

SIGNATURE RESUMES

P.O. Box 7151
Rochester, MN 55903
(507) 282-7787

Specializes in serving business and technical professionals. Client interview, resume writing, editing, layout and formatting. Four-color self-promotion materials. Cover letters, disk storage. Call for appointment and pricing.

RESUME PREPARATION SERVICES

WESTERN WISCONSIN

BURGER & BURGER CREATIVE SERVICES
1321 Stout Road
Menomonie, WI 54751
(715) 235-8786

Offers client consultation, resume writing, layout, formatting, and printouts. Cover letters. Disk storage on Apple or Mac computer. Call for appointment and fees.

CEDARWOOD SECRETARIAL SERVICE
306 So. Barstow Street
Barstow Court
Eau Claire, WI 54701
(715) 835-2702—Phone/Fax

Free initial visit. Services include resume writing, layout, formatting, and printouts. Also provides cover letters, disk storage, and one-to-one coaching. Packages range from $15—55. Call for appointment.

COMPUTER SERVICES PLUS
River Falls, WI 54022
(715) 425-8773   Fax—(715) 425-2383

Free initial visit. Resume writing, layout, formatting, printouts. Cover letters, disk storage. Resume packages start at approximately $30. Call for appointment.

EMPLOYEE DEVELOPMENT SERVICES OF WISCONSIN
534 Water
Eau Claire, WI 54703
(715) 834-8326   Fax—(715) 834-8398

Services include client interview, resume writing, layout, formatting, printouts. Cover letters. Call for information and fees.

School Career Centers

Technical Colleges
Community Colleges
Universities and Liberal Arts Colleges
Area High Schools

If you think that schools are only good for earning degrees or diplomas, it's time to do your homework. Universities, community colleges, technical schools, high schools, and community education departments provide a wide range of services to job seekers, career-changers, would-be students, and graduates. Many offer opportunities to explore interests, abilities, new careers, or to receive expert job search counseling.

School-based career centers are generally accessible to the public. Some services (mostly colleges) are available only to current students or alumni. If you are primarily looking for career guidance, including testing and interpretation, school career services are exceptional values, typically offered for free or at low cost.

The school career centers listed on the following pages are located throughout Minnesota and western Wisconsin.

SCHOOL CAREER CENTERS

TWIN CITIES

ANOKA-RAMSEY COMMUNITY COLLEGE
11200 Mississippi Blvd. N.W.
Coon Rapids, MN 55433
(612) 427-2600   Fax—(612) 422-3341

Open to the public. Provides career assessment, interpretation, individual counseling, resource center, classes, workshops. Fees vary.

AUGSBURG COLLEGE CAREER SERVICES
2211 Riverside Avenue
Minneapolis, MN 55454
(612) 330-1162   Fax—(612) 330-1649

Open to current students and alumni. Provides individual career counseling, testing, job-search coaching, resource center, job hotline. Free.

COLLEGE OF ST. CATHERINE
Career Development

2004 Randolph Avenue
St. Paul, MN 55105
(612) 690-6510

Open to current students and alumnae. Provides career planning, job-search counseling, resume development, resource library, interest/career testing, job leads. Call for appointment. Free to students and alumnae for limited time; thereafter, $25 per hour for individual counseling.

DAKOTA COUNTY TECHNICAL COLLEGE
Career Assessment Center

1300 E. 145th Street
Rosemount, MN 55068
(612) 423-8409

Open to the public. Offers career assessment, testing, individual/group counseling, job-search coaching. Also provides job leads, resource library, workshops, support group. Call for appointment. Use of resource center is free. Additional fees apply for testing, classes and workshops.

HAMLINE UNIVERSITY
Career Development Center
1536 Hewitt Avenue
St. Paul, MN 55104
(612) 641-2302

Open and free to students and alumni for two years following graduation. Alumni served on space-available basis. Offers career planning, job-search counseling, resume development, resource library, workshops, job leads. Call for appointment and fees.

HENNEPIN TECHNICAL COLLEGE
Counseling Services

Brooklyn Park Campus
9000 Brooklyn Blvd.
Brooklyn Park, MN 55445
(612) 425-3800

Eden Prairie Campus
9200 Flying Cloud Drive
Eden Prairie, MN 55347
(612) 944-2222

Open to the public. Offers career and vocational counseling, financial aid counseling, testing and assessment. Open weekday and evenings. Call for appointment or drop in. Free or low-cost.

HOPKINS ADULT CAREER CENTER
Hopkins Senior High School
2400 Lindbergh Drive
Minnetonka, MN 55343
(612) 933-9248   Fax—(612) 933-9382

Open to adults on Tuesday evenings from 6:45—9:15 p.m. from September through May. Low-cost career assessment tests and interpretation ranging from $5—$25. Computerized vocational data bank, resource library. Drop in or call. Free consultation staff on duty.

SCHOOL CAREER CENTERS

LAKEWOOD COMMUNITY COLLEGE
Career Clinic

3401 Century Avenue
White Bear Lake, MN 55110
(612) 779-3370   Fax—(612) 779-3417

Open to the public. Provides career planning, interest testing, job-search workshops, individual counseling, resource library, resume and interviewing coaching. Call for appointment. Fees: $30 for interest testing and consultation; $87 for workshop.

LIFEWORKS
Bloomington Education Center

8900 Portland Ave. So.   5701 Normandale Road, Rm 333
Bloomington, MN 55420   Edina, MN 55424
(612) 885-8553   (612) 928-1416

Open to the public. Targeted to unemployed or underemployed individuals seeking improved positions. Offers individualized career planning and development, workshops, computerized career information, skills for getting and keeping a job, resource library. Call for appointment. Free to eligible participants.

MACALESTER COLLEGE
Career Development Center

1600 Grand Avenue
St. Paul, MN 55105
(612) 696-6384   Fax—(612) 696-6131

Open to current students and alumni. Individual career counseling, testing, resume development, resource library, internships, computerized job-seeking skills program, job postings. Call or write for appointment. No charge to students or alumni for one year after graduation.

This chapter continues on the following page.

METROPOLITAN STATE UNIVERSITY
Resource Center

730 Hennepin Avenue
Minneapolis, MN 55403
(612) 341-7580

700 E. 7th Street
St. Paul, MN 55106
(612) 772-7633

Open to the public. Services include career testing, personal career counseling, computer-assisted resources. Call for appointment. Free with fees for interest testing.

MINNEAPOLIS COMMUNITY COLLEGE
Career Center

1501 Hennepin Avenue
Minneapolis, MN 55403-1779
(612) 341-7040

Open to the public. Computerized career exploration program. Also offers career exploration classes at a fee. Call for appointment.

MINNETONKA ADULT CAREER CENTER
Minnetonka High School Community Services

18301 Highway 7
Minnetonka, MN 55345
(612) 470-3450

For adults in career transition. Open to the public on drop-in basis most Monday from 7—9 p.m. throughout school year. Offers interest, career testing, consultation, job-search and resume assistance. Resource library offers computerized career data. Free except for test scoring.

NORMANDALE COMMUNITY COLLEGE
Career Services

9700 France Ave. So.
Bloomington, MN 55431
(612) 832-6350   Fax—832-6571

Open to the public. Provides individual and group career assessment and testing, workshops, job-search coaching. Fees range from $8-$70. No charge to access career library, software and Job Service Job Bank.

SCHOOL CAREER CENTERS

NORTH HENNEPIN COMMUNITY COLLEGE
Career Center

7411 85th Ave. No.
Brooklyn Park, MN 55445
(612) 424-0703

Open to the public but targeted to students or prospective students. Services include use of interactive computer program for self-assessment and career information, access to Job Service Job Bank and resource library. Call for appointment. Free.

NORTHEAST METRO TECHNICAL COLLEGE
Career Counseling

3300 Century Ave. No..
White Bear Lake, MN 55110
(612) 770-2351   Fax—(612) 779-5810

Open to the public. Provides career assessment, testing, individual counseling, access to job bank, resource materials. Call for appointment. Services are free; career testing may be additional cost.

ROSEVILLE AREA IND. SCHOOL DISTRICT
Career Services

1910 W. County Road B, Rm 124
Roseville, MN 55113
(612) 631-2809   Fax—(612) 631-2544

Open to the public. Offers career assessment, vocational testing, resource library, job-search coaching, resume/interview preparation. Free.

SAINT PAUL TECHNICAL COLLEGE
Student Services Career Center

235 Marshall Avenue
St. Paul, MN 55102
(612) 221-1370   Fax—(612) 221-1416

Open to the public. Provides career assessment, videotapes, and computer programs for career exploration. Job placement assistance from staff and State Job Service representative. Free. Drop in.

UNIVERSITY OF MINNESOTA
Carlson School of Management
CAREER SERVICES CENTER
190 Humphrey Center
271 19th Ave. So.
Minneapolis, MN 55455
(612) 624-0011   Fax—(612) 626-1822

Open to Carlson School of Management students and alumni. Offers career planning, job-search coaching, resource library, seminars, job leads, job fairs, internships, resume referral service. Call for appointment. Free to current students; $25/6 months for alumni.

UNIVERSITY OF MINNESOTA
Dept. of Counseling, Continuing Education & Extension (CEE)
314 Nolte Center, 315 Pillsbury Drive S.E.
Minneapolis, MN 55455
(612) 625-2500   Fax—(612) 625-5364

Open to individuals considering further education at the University through CEE. Offers career counseling, testing, workshops. Call for information and fees.

UNIVERSITY OF MINNESOTA
College of Agriculture
CAREER SERVICES OFFICE
272 Coffey Hall, 1420 Eckles Avenue
St. Paul, MN 55108
(612) 624-2710   Fax—(612) 625-1260

Open to U of M students and alumni. Services include individualized counseling, resume preparation, networking opportunities, resource materials, job leads, career fair. Call for appointment. Free.

SCHOOL CAREER CENTERS

UNIVERSITY OF MINNESOTA
College of Biological Sciences
CAREER INFORMATION CENTER
217 Snyder Hall, 1475 Gortner Avenue
St. Paul, MN 55108
(612) 624-9270   Fax—(612) 624-2785

Open to individuals interested in biology careers. Offers workshops, resume-writing assistance, resource library, prospective employer information. Resume referral service for current students and alumni. Drop in. Free.

UNIVERSITY OF MINNESOTA
College of Education
EDUCATION STUDENT AFFAIRS OFFICE
40 Wulling Hall
Minneapolis, MN 55455
(612) 625-6501   Fax—(612) 626-1580

Open to individuals interested in education careers. Provides career planning, job-search counseling, resume preparation, resource library, workshops, job leads, international teaching opportunities. Call for appointment. Most services are free.

UNIVERSITY OF MINNESOTA
College of Human Ecology
CAREER SERVICES CENTER
68 McNeal Hall, 1985 Buford Avenue
St. Paul, MN 55108
(612) 624-6762   Fax—(612) 625-5767

Free to CHE students and alumni. Offers career planning, job-search counseling, resume development, resource library, seminars, job leads. Call for appointment.

This chapter continues on the following page.

UNIVERSITY OF MINNESOTA
College of Liberal Arts
CAREER DEVELOPMENT OFFICE
345 Fraser Hall, 106 Pleasant Street
Minneapolis, MN 55455
(612) 624-7505

Open to CLA students and alumni. Services include career planning, job-search counseling, resume preparation, resource library, seminars. Call or drop in. Free to students and alumni for one year following graduation; thereafter $15 per session.

UNIVERSITY OF MINNESOTA
Hubert H. Humphrey Institute of Public Affairs
301 19th Ave. So.
Minneapolis, MN 55455
(612) 625-2847   Fax—(612) 625-6351

Open only to Humphrey students and alumni. Assistance with career planning, job-search skills, resume development, resource materials, job leads. Call for appointment. Free.

UNIVERSITY OF MINNESOTA
Institute of Technology
CAREER CENTER
50 Lind Hall, 207 Church St. S.E.
Minneapolis, MN 55455
(612) 624-4090   Fax—(612) 626-0261

Open to current students and alumni. Free career planning and placement services, job-search and resume assistance. Resource library, seminars, job leads, resume referral service. Call for appointment.

SCHOOL CAREER CENTERS

UNIVERSITY OF MINNESOTA
University Counseling and Consulting Services
CAREER DEVELOPMENT CENTER
192 Pillsbury Drive S.E., 109 Eddy Hall
Minneapolis, MN 55455
(612) 624-8344   Fax—(612) 624-0207

Primarily open and free to prospective and current students; non-students served on availability basis. Services include career assessment, testing, individual/group career counseling, resource center, workshops. Call for information and fees.

UNIVERSITY OF MINNESOTA
Vocational Assessment Clinic
N555 Elliott Hall
75 East River Road
Minneapolis, MN 55455
(612) 625-1519

Open to adults who are not full-time students at the University of Minnesota. Offers vocational assessment, career planning, individual counseling. Call for appointment. Individual counseling fees, $225-$250.

UNIVERSITY OF ST. THOMAS
Counseling and Career Services
350 Murray-Herrick
2115 Summit Avenue
St. Paul, MN 55105
(612) 962-6761

Open to current students and alumni. Provides career planning, resume preparation, job-search coaching, resource library, interest/career testing, job leads. Call for appointment. Free one year after graduation; thereafter $25/hour or $95/year.

This chapter continues on the following page.

MINNESOTA JOB SEEKER'S SOURCEBOOK

NORTHERN MINNESOTA

BEMIDJI STATE UNIVERSITY
Career Services

1500 Birchmont Drive N.E.
Bemidji, MN 56607
(218) 755-2038   Fax—(218) 755-4115

Open to the public but targeted to current or prospective students. Offers career assessment, job-search coaching, resume assistance, job placement, resource library, credential services, job vacancy bulletins, job fairs. Call or drop in. Fees for some services.

BRAINERD COMMUNITY COLLEGE
Career Center

501 W. College Drive
Brainerd, MN 56401
(218) 828-2525   Fax—(218) 828-2710

Open to the public but targeted to students. Provides career assessment, testing, resource library, job-search coaching, resume and interview assistance, career planning classes, job leads. Also offers vocational/college information. Call for appointment. Free.

BRAINERD-STAPLES TECHNICAL COLLEGE
Career Placement Department

1830 Airport Road
Staples, MN 56479
(218) 894-1168   Fax—(218) 894-2546

Open only to current students and alumni. Offers career assessment and testing, workshops, resource library, job-search coaching, job leads. Call for appointment. Free.

SCHOOL CAREER CENTERS

COLLEGE OF ST. SCHOLASTICA
Student Development Center

1200 Kenwood
Duluth, MN 55811
(218) 723-6085   Fax—(218) 723-6290

Open only to enrolled students and alumni. Offers career counseling and testing, job-search coaching, resource library, job bank, career classes, credential maintenance and mailing. Call for appointment. Free.

DULUTH COMMUNITY COLLEGE

1309 Rice Lake Road
Duluth, MN 55811
(218) 723-4796   Fax—(218) 723-4921

Open to the public. Services include career assessment and testing, workshops, resource library. Call for an appointment or drop in. Free.

DULUTH TECHNICAL COLLEGE
Counseling Department

2101 Trinity Road
Duluth, MN 55811
(218) 722-2801   Fax—(218) 722-2899

Open to the public. Offers career assessment and testing, workshops, resource library, job placement (for grads only), women's resource center. Call for an appointment. Free.

FOND DU LAC COMMUNITY COLLEGE
College Center

2101 14th Street
Cloquet, MN 55720
(218) 879-0800   Fax—(218) 879-0814

Open to the public but targeted to enrolled students. Provides career assessment, resource library, resume and interview assistance, career exploration/job-search classes. Call for appointment and fees.

This chapter continues on the following page.

MINNESOTA JOB SEEKER'S SOURCEBOOK

HIBBING COMMUNITY COLLEGE
Career Center
1515 E. 25th Street
Hibbing, MN 55746
(218) 262-6700   Fax—(218) 262-6717

Open to the public but targeted to enrolled students. Services include career assessment, testing, vocational software, resource library. Call for appointment. Free or low-cost.

ITASCA COMMUNITY COLLEGE
1851 E. Hwy. 169
Grand Rapids, MN 55744
(218) 327-4460   Fax—(218) 327-4350

Open to the public but targeted to current students. Offers career testing, resource library. Call for an appointment. Free.

RAINY RIVER COMMUNITY COLLEGE
Career Center
1501 Highway 71
International Falls, MN 56649
(218) 285-7722   Fax—(218) 285-2239

Open to the public but targeted to enrolled students. Offers career assessment, testing, resume and interviewing assistance, workshops, career development classes, resource library. Call for appointment. Fees for courses and workshops.

RANGE TECHNICAL COLLEGE

EVELETH CAMPUS
1100 Industrial Park Dr.
Eveleth, MN 55734
(218) 744-3302   (800) 345-2884

HIBBING CAMPUS
2900 E. Beltline
Hibbing, MN 55746
(218) 262-7200

Open to the public. Offers career assessment and testing, workshops, job placement, resource library, job-search coaching, job leads, supplemental services, tutoring, minority vocational advising. Call for appointment and fees.

SCHOOL CAREER CENTERS

UNIVERSITY OF MINNESOTA—CROOKSTON
Counseling and Career Center

Bede Hall, Rm 106
Crookston, MN 56716
(218) 281-8585

Open to the public but targeted to enrolled students and graduates. Services include career assessment and testing, job-search coaching, resume and interview preparation, resource library, job leads. Call for appointment or drop in. Fees start at $20.

UNIVERSITY OF MINNESOTA—DULUTH
Career Services

255 Darland Administration Building
10 University Drive
Duluth, MN 55812
(218) 726-7985

Open only to UMD students. Offers career assessment, testing, job-search coaching, resume assistance, workshops, job placement, resource library. Call for appointment. Fees for testing, placement credentials, job-vacancy bulletin.

CENTRAL MINNESOTA

ALEXANDRIA TECHNICAL COLLEGE
Career Planning and Assessment Center

1601 Jefferson
Alexandria, MN 56308
(800) 253-9884   Fax—(612) 762-4501

Open to the public but targeted to students. Offers career assessment and testing, job placement, resource library, job-search coaching, retraining. Call for appointment. Free.

This chapter continues on the following page.

COLLEGE OF ST. BENEDICT
Career Services

37 So. College Avenue
St. Joseph, MN 56374
(612) 363-5707

Open only to current students and alumni. Offers career and job-search counseling, interest/personality testing, computer-based inventories. Publishes job vacancy bulletin. Call for appointment and fees.

FERGUS FALLS COMMUNITY COLLEGE
Career Information Center

1414 College Way
Fergus Falls, MN 56537
(218) 739-7555   Fax—(218) 739-7475

Open to the public. Services include career assessment, testing, workshops, resource library, job-search coaching, computerized career information. Free for students; $5 one-time fee to community.

NORTHWEST TECHNICAL COLLEGE
Placement Services

405 S.W. Colfax
Wadena, MN 56482
(218) 631-3530   (800) 247-2007 ext. 2007   Fax—(218) 631-9207

Open only to students and graduates. Offers career assessment, job-search coaching, resource library, workshops, job placement, computerized career information. Call for appointment. Free.

PINE TECHNICAL COLLEGE

1100 Fourth Street
Pine City, MN 55063
(612) 629-6764

Open to the public. Provides career assessment, job placement, workshops, resource library, job-search coaching. Access to Job Bank and Minnesota Career Information Service. Call for an appointment. Free.

SCHOOL CAREER CENTERS

ST. CLOUD STATE UNIVERSITY
Career Services

AS-101, 720 So. Fourth Avenue
St. Cloud, MN 56301
(612) 255-2151

Open to the public. Assistance with resumes, interviewing and job-search skills. Offers resource library with computer database indexing job opportunities across the country. Job vacancy bulletin. Call for appointment. Free.

ST. CLOUD TECHNICAL COLLEGE
Placement Office

1540 Northway Drive
St. Cloud, MN 56303
(612) 654-5000

Open only to current students and alumni. Provides career planning, job-search counseling, resume development. Assistance with networking, interviewing, negotiating skills. Resource library, job leads and annual job fair. Call for appointment. Free.

ST. JOHN'S UNIVERSITY
Counseling and Career Services

Collegeville, MN 56321-2000
(612) 363-3791

Open only to current students and alumni. Offers career counseling, interest assessment, resource library, access to corporate information databases. Call for appointment and fees.

This chapter continues on the following page.

SOUTHERN MINNESOTA

AUSTIN COMMUNITY COLLEGE
Counseling and Career Center

1600 8th Ave. N.W.
Austin, MN 55912
(507) 433-0505   Fax—(507) 433-0515

Open to the public. Services include career assessment and testing, job-search coaching, workshops, job bank, job placement, resource library. Call for appointment. Free, but fees charged for some tests.

FARIBAULT SENIOR HIGH SCHOOL
Career Resource Center

330 9th Ave. S.W.
Faribault, MN 55021
(507) 334-5527

Open to the public. Offers career assessment, vocational testing, job-search coaching, resource library. Call for appointment. Free.

HASTINGS SENIOR HIGH SCHOOL
Career Resource Center

1000 11th St. W.
Hastings, MN 55033-2597
(612) 438-0753   Fax—(612) 437-7332

Open to the public, weekdays throughout school year. Offers career resource library with computerized career information, vocational/college catalogs, career publications. Call for appointment. Free.

SCHOOL CAREER CENTERS

MINNESOTA RIVERLAND TECHNICAL COLLEGE

Reach Center
1926 College View Road S.E.
Rochester, MN 55904
(507) 285-7074

Career Center
1900 N.W. 8th Avenue
Austin, MN 55912
(507) 433-0600   (800) 247-5039

Career Resource Center
1225 S.W. Third Street
Faribault, MN 55021
(507) 334-3965   Fax—(507) 332-5888

Open to the public from September through May. Services vary by location but may include career assessment, testing, job-search coaching, workshops, resource library. Also coaches single parents, displaced homemakers, and individuals pursuing non-traditional careers. Call for appointment. Free.

OWATONNA SENIOR HIGH SCHOOL
Community Career Center

333 E. School Street
Owatonna, MN 55060
(507) 451-4710

Open to the public. Offers job-search coaching, career resource library and computerized career/vocational information. Call for appointment. Free.

ROCHESTER COMMUNITY COLLEGE
Counseling Center

851 30th Ave. S.E.
Rochester, MN 55904
(507) 285-7260   Fax—(507) 285-7496

Offers career assessment, testing, job-search coaching, workshops only to current students. Resource library is open to the public. Call for appointment. Free.

This chapter continues on the following page.

ST. OLAF COLLEGE
Career Development Center

1520 St. Olaf Avenue
Northfield, MN 55057
(507) 646-3268

Open to current students and alumni. Provides career assessment, testing, job-search coaching, job leads, internship opportunities, resource library. Call for appointment. Free.

SOUTH CENTRAL TECHNICAL COLLEGE

LIBRARY RESOURCE CENTER
2200 Tech Drive
Albert Lea, MN 56007
(507) 373-0656

PLACEMENT OFFICE
1920 Lee Blvd.
North Mankato, MN 56002
(507) 625-3441   (800) 722-9359

Open to the public but targeted to students. Offers career assessment, testing, job-search coaching, access to Job Service Job Bank. Drop in. Free.

SOUTHWEST STATE UNIVERSITY
Career Services

Bellows 268
1501 State Street
Marshall, MN 56258
(507) 537-6221   Fax—(507) 537-6200

Open to the public. Services include career assessment, vocational testing, job-search coaching, resume/interview preparation, job placement, workshops, resource library. Drop in. Free.

SCHOOL CAREER CENTERS

SOUTHWESTERN TECHNICAL COLLEGE
Career Center

1011 First St. W.
Canby, MN 56220
(612) 223-7252   (800) 658-2535

1593 11th Avenue
Granite Falls, MN 56241
(612) 564-4511   (800) 657-3247

401 W. Street
Jackson, MN 56143
(507) 847-3320   (800) 658-2522

P.O. Box 250
1314 No. Hiawatha
Pipestone, MN 56164
(507) 825-5471   (800) 658-2330

Open to the public. Services vary by location but generally include career assessment, testing, resource library, job leads. Call for appointment. Free.

WINONA STATE UNIVERSITY
Career Training and Placement

110 Gildemeister Hall
Winona, MN 55987
(507) 457-5340   Fax—(507) 457-5516

Open only to graduating students and alumni. Offers job-search coaching, job leads, resource library, job fairs. Call for appointment. Alumni fees: $25 per year.

WINONA TECHNICAL COLLEGE
Student Services Center

P.O. Box 409
1250 Homer Road
Winona, MN 55987
(507) 454-4600   (800) 372-8164   Fax—(507) 452-1564

Open to the public. Assists with career assessment and job-search skills. Offers testing, job leads and placement, resource library. Call for an appointment. Free.

This chapter continues on the following page.

WESTERN WISCONSIN

CHIPPEWA VALLEY TECHNICAL COLLEGE

MENOMONIE
Open to the public.
403 Technology Park Drive E.
Menomonie, WI 54751
(715) 232-2685

EAU CLAIRE
Open to the public but targeted to enrolled students.
620 W. Clairemont Avenue
Eau Claire, WI 54701
(715) 833-6257   Fax—(715) 833-6470

RIVER FALLS
Must be age 18 and not enrolled in another school.
P.O. Box 496, 715 No. Main St.
River Falls, MN 54022
(715) 425-3301

Services vary by location but may include career assessment, testing, resource library, job-search coaching. Call for information and fees.

UNIVERSITY OF WISCONSIN—EAU CLAIRE
Career Planning and Placement

Schofield Hall, Rm 230
Eau Claire, WI 54702-4004
(715) 836-5358   Fax—(715) 836-4023

Resource library is free and open to the public. Other career services including testing and job placement are targeted to enrolled students and graduates. Call for hours. Free.

UNIVERSITY OF WISCONSIN—LA CROSSE
Career Resource Center

Second Floor, Wilder Hall
La Crosse, WI 54601
(608) 785-8514   Fax—(608) 785-8518

Open to public. Offers job-search coaching, resume/interview preparation, resource center, workshops, job-listing bulletins. Drop in. Free.

SCHOOL CAREER CENTERS

UNIVERSITY OF WISCONSIN—RIVER FALLS
Career Services
River Falls, WI 54022
(715) 425-3572   Fax—(715) 425-4487

Open to the public but targeted to enrolled students and alumni. Assistance with job-search skills, resume/interview preparation, job leads. Career resource library. Call for information and fees.

UNIVERSITY OF WISCONSIN—STOUT
Placement and Co-op Services
103 Administration Building
Menomonie, WI 54751
(715) 232-1601   Fax—(715) 232-3595

Open to the public but targeted to enrolled students and alumni. Offers job-search coaching, resume/interview preparation, job-listing bulletins, resource library, workshops. Call for appointment. Free.

UNIVERSITY OF WISCONSIN—SUPERIOR
Career Center
1800 Grand Avenue
Old Main 134
Superior, WI 54880
(715) 394-8305

Open only to UW—Superior students, alumni and prospective students. Provides career assessment, testing, job-search coaching, resume assistance, job leads, resource library, workshops, job vacancy bulletins. Call for appointment. Services start at $10.

WISCONSIN INDIANHEAD TECHNICAL COLLEGE
600 No. 21st Street
Superior, WI 54880
(715) 394-6677   Fax—(715) 394-3771

Open to the public. Offers career assessment, testing, job-search skills, resume assistance, job placement, resource library, workshops. Call for appointment and fees.

RESEARCH RESOURCES

In a tight job market, one way to stand above your competition is to gather facts like a pro. A little roll-up-your-sleeves research will provide you with current information about potential employers, industry outlooks, authoritative dos and don'ts of the job-search, salary surveys, and up-and-coming careers.

It's no surprise that the library is the best place to start your research. Public, business, academic, and career libraries offer a gold mine of resources to job seekers. How-to books, business directories, vocational guides, job opportunity newsletters, magazine articles, pamphlets, library clipping services, and instructional cassette tapes are a sampling of the resources available.

Most libraries have vocational sections where you'll find popular books on how to organize your job hunt or improve your resume. Look in the non-circulating reference collection for information about specific companies. Here you can find business directories, annual reports, and "Who's Who" guides. Check the periodical collection for trade and professional publications which may offer late-breaking news about your field or industry.

The library can also introduce you to some new and surprisingly powerful resources. On-line computer databases—some accessible for free at area libraries—allow you to browse through national job banks, industry reports, and more, at the touch of a keystroke.

For a quick and focused start, meet with a reference librarian in either the sociology or business department. Explain the sort of information you need, and don't be shy. Librarians can be immensely helpful. Self-directed researchers should start by checking headings like "Job Hunting," "Employment," "Resumes," and "Job Applications" in card catalogs, periodical guides, pamphlet files, or microfiche indexes.

Serious researchers should look beyond the corner public library. Locate the library in your system with the largest reference collection, and start your research there.

Most college and university libraries are also open to the public (although you may not be able to check out materials here unless you have a student I.D. or alumni card). In addition, consider the materials available at career resource centers or counseling offices located at colleges, universities, social service agencies, employment assistance centers or private businesses. Many of these centers subscribe to hard-to-find specialty career publications.

JOB-SEEKING ON-LINE

A decade ago, who would have thought you could instantly access huge banks of information from the comfort of your home PC. Today, there are hundreds of on-line databases and bulletin boards where you can gather current information on job or career-related topics, or chat with other job seekers.

If you're new to computer bulletin boards or database research, several books can teach you the ropes, and direct you to appropriate on-line services. Check your local library or bookstore for these directories: Whole Earth Online Almanac, (Brady); The Electronic Traveler, (Windcrest Books); The Gale Directory of Databases, (Gale Research); Online Factbook, (Digital Information Group).

Galacticomm, maker of bulletin board software, publishes a free guide to over 800 public bulletin board systems in the U.S. and Canada. To get one, call (305) 583-5990.

MINNESOTA JOB SEEKER'S SOURCEBOOK

COMMERCIAL ON-LINE DATABASES

Commercial databases are quick routes to vast storehouses of information. Before you start, clarify the type of information you're after. Charges can add up quickly after you log on. For most commercial services, expect to pay an initial sign-up fee, along with monthly, hourly, and long-distance phone charges. Call the toll-free numbers listed below for access information.

AMERICA ONLINE   (800) 827-6364
News, weather, sports, stock quotes.

COMPUSERVE   (800) 848-8199
Libraries of business and other news.

GENIE   (800) 638-9636
News, consumer information, financial services.

PRODIGY   (800) 776-3449
News, business, travel, education.

BRS AFTER DARK   (800) 955-0906.
Databases on the environment, science, and medicine.

DATA-STAR   (800) 221-7754
Contains 300 databases of information on international marketplace.

DIALOG   (800) 334-2564
Contains 450 databases on businesses, science, technology and millions of domestic and international companies.

DOW JONES NEWS/RETRIEVAL   (800) 522-3567
Full text of Wall Street Journal, Barron's, Business & Finance Report and American Demographics.

NEWSNET   (800) 345-1301
Access to 600 business newsletters and 20 worldwide news wires.

NEXIS AND LEXIS   (800) 227-4908
Nexis provides access to 3,000 databases with newspapers, news wires, magazines, financial services and more. Lexis is the legal equivalent.

RESEARCH RESOURCES

BULLETIN BOARD SYSTEM (BBS)
Minnesota Department of Jobs & Training

(612) 297-7343—BBS
(612) 296-6545—Voice Assistance

This free on-line service, by the Department of Jobs & Training, Research and Statistics Office, provides access to labor market information and the department's latest news releases. All files may be downloaded. Call for a brochure describing the files available and how to access the system. Also provided is a bulletin board allowing users to communicate.

CAREER INFORMATION

MINNESOTA CAREER INFORMATION SYSTEM
Minnesota Department of Education

932 Capitol Square Building, 550 Cedar Street
St. Paul, MN 55101
(612) 296-3653

The MCIS, available at many technical colleges, libraries, and other locations, is a database with extensive occupational and educational information. The MCIS describes hundreds of occupations, and the training or education needed to get into each field. Also included is national school and scholarship information, tips for job seekers, local resources for starting a business, and more. Free.

COMMUNITY PROFILES

METROPOLITAN COUNCIL DATA CENTER
Mears Park Centre
230 East Fifth Street
St. Paul, Minnesota 55101
(612) 291-8140

The Metropolitan Council publishes reports about the economy and other data about the greater Twin Cities metro area. Call or write for a free publications directory.

RESEARCH SERVICES

DODGE BUSINESS RESEARCH CONSULTING
3208 W. Lake Street, Suite 110
Minneapolis, MN 55416
(612) 525-7372

Research service targeted to management and executive-level job seekers, and others seeking customized computer database searches of companies, or other information. Fees start at $25 to search 1,100 global business magazines, trade journals, regional business newspapers. Client receives citations only, and must provide specific company names.

INFORM
Minneapolis Public Library
300 Nicollet Mall
Minneapolis, MN
(612) 372-6636

Research service, open to the public, conducts customized searches on all topics at $60 per hour with a 15-minute minimum. Call for an appointment or drop in.

BUSINESS REFERENCE

JAMES J. HILL REFERENCE LIBRARY
80 West Fourth Street
St. Paul, MN 55102
(612) 227-9531

This private reference library is home to an impressive non-circulating collection of business resources. In addition, the library offers free access by reservation, to computer databases such as National Trade Data Bank, Compact Disclosure, Star Tribune on Newsbank, ABI/Inform on disk, Predicast F & S plus text (U.S.), Dunn's Business Locator, Dunn's Million Dollar on disk, and Dunn's Middle Market on disk. Reference librarians can also search other databases for a fee. Open Monday through Saturday

CHAPTER FOUR

WHERE TO FIND EMPLOYMENT LEADS

I f it's time to get serious about finding a job, listen up. There are more ways to track down "positions available" than waiting for the right job to surface in the Sunday want ads. In this chapter, you will find resources that lead to actual job vacancies or potential employers. These resources include employer-sponsored job hotlines, search firms, employment agencies, recruitment publications, and job-lead services like job banks and resume referral services.

Many professional associations also provide job leads to their members, or to members of their respective industries. See Chapter Five for a sampling of networking associations.

Remember: many jobs are never advertised, and most people — about 85%—find work through networking. But don't let these statistics deter you. A good strategy requires that you use every tool available to find the right job match.

Job Hotlines

A telephone, a legal pad and a sharp pencil may be all you need to instantly access current information about job vacancies. Job hotlines sponsored by local corporations, government personnel departments, and other organizations, provide free recorded messages that highlight the duties, salary ranges, application procedures, and other requirements for positions available.

The amount and type of information provided varies between organizations. Most listings are updated weekly.

Here are some other quick tips when accessing a job hotline:

◆ Have pen and paper in hand: Information comes quickly.

◆ Some job hotlines require the use of a touch-tone phone, but options are generally provided for rotary phone callers.

◆ Unless you don't mind hitting your re-dial button, call popular numbers like the Federal Jobline, for example, on evenings or weekends.

◆ Hotline numbers change frequently. If you reach a number that is no longer in service, call the organization's human resources department and ask for updated information.

JOB HOTLINES

All job hotline sponsors are located in the Twin Cities metropolitan area unless otherwise noted in listing.

ACCOUNTING ACTION LINE
(612) 773-0648

Job hotline. Recorded listing of current accounting positions at Accounting Placement Registry, a Minneapolis search firm. Information includes job description and salary range.

AETNA HEALTH PLANS
(612) 897-2574

Job hotline. Recorded message describes position titles for current openings, and the application process.

AMERICAN ASSOCIATION OF LAW LIBRARIES
(312) 939-7877

Job hotline. Recorded message includes job descriptions, locations, requirements, salary ranges, and application instructions for job opportunities throughout U.S. Updated weekly.

ANOKA COUNTY
(612) 422-7498

Job hotline. Recorded message provides detailed job descriptions, requirements, and salary range. Updated as postings become available.

AUGSBURG COLLEGE
(612) 330-1414
(612) 330-1425—Business/Liberal Arts
(612) 330-1426—Education

Job hotlines. Recorded information describes current openings, job descriptions, requirements, and application instructions.

This chapter continues on the following page.

BANKERS SYSTEMS—ST. CLOUD
(612) 251-6114

Job hotline. Recorded message describes current job descriptions, requirements, and application instructions.

BARR ENGINEERING
(612) 832-2600

Ask for job hotline. Recorded message describes current job openings and application instructions.

BLUE CROSS/BLUE SHIELD OF MINNESOTA
(612) 456-8020

Job hotline. Recorded message includes job description, requirements, and application procedure. Updated weekly.

CAREER AMERICA CONNECTION
U.S. Office of Personnel Management
(912) 757-3000

Job hotline. Offers College Hotline and General Hotline. Recordings list current jobs available, nationwide, with the Federal Government providing locations, salary range, and application instructions.

CERNET FREE
(612) 377-8141

Job information resource for the gay and lesbian community. Operator provides current job descriptions, requirements, locations, salary range, and application process. Answered M—F, 8 a.m.—8 p.m. Weekends, noon—6 p.m.

JOB HOTLINES

CITY LINE'S EMPLOYMENT DIRECTORY
(612) 645-6060 cat. 5627 (JOBS)

Job hotline. Recorded messages provide job titles, employers, job descriptions, salary ranges, requirements, and application procedures. Instructions explain how to select job listings in these areas below. Touch-tone phone is required.

1919—Hubbard Broadcasting
2500—University of Minnesota
5628—Professional / Administrative
5629—Financial / Accounting
5630—Sales / Marketing
5631—Computers / Technical / Engineering
5632—Office Support / Clerical
5633—Secretarial / Typing
5634—Word Processing
5635—Health Care
5636—Industrial / Construction / Labor
5637—Driving / Transportation
5638—Restaurant / Food Service
5639—Miscellaneous
5640—Part-time / Seasonal
5641—Temporary Positions

CITY OF MINNEAPOLIS
(612) 673-2666

Job hotline. Recorded information provides job description, requirements, and application procedure. Updated bi-weekly.

CITY OF ST. PAUL
(612) 266-6502

Job hotline. Recorded message includes job description, salary range, requirements and application procedure.

This chapter continues on the following page.

COLLEGE OF ST. CATHERINE
(612) 690-6425

Job hotline. Recorded listings of job descriptions, requirements, and application instructions. Updated weekly.

DAHLBERG
(612) 520-9500 ext. 115

Job hotline. Recorded listings of current job descriptions, requirements, and application procedure.

DAKOTA COUNTY
(612) 438-4473

Job hotline. Recorded message describes weekly postings of Dakota County jobs. Recording provides job title and salary range.

DAMARK INTERNATIONAL
(612) 531-4562

Job hotline. Recorded information lists current job openings and application instructions.

DATACARD
(612) 931-1990   (800) 328-4254

Job hotline. Recorded message provides job descriptions, requirements, and application process. Updated weekly.

DAYTON'S EMPLOYMENT
(612) 375-4288

Job hotline. Recorded message provides job descriptions, requirements, location, and application procedure. Updated weekly.

DELUXE CORPORATION
(612) 481-4100

Job hotline. Recorded message includes current job descriptions, requirements, and application process.

JOB HOTLINES

DIAL-A-JOB/DIAL-AN-INTERN
National Association for Interpretation

(303) 491-7410   (303) 491-6784

Job hotline. Recorded information describes a small number of environmental positions and internships nationwide. Updated weekly.

EDEN PRAIRIE SCHOOL DISTRICT

(612) 937-1650

Ask for hotline. Recorded information about teaching and other positions available at Eden Prairie school district.

EDITORIAL FREELANCE ASSOCIATION

(212) 929-5411   (212) 807-4174

Job hotline. The public can access this hotline to hear recorded general information about freelance opportunities nationwide, but only members can receive detailed descriptions of positions. Updated weekly. Membership, $20 per year.

FAIRVIEW SOUTHDALE HOSPITAL

(612) 924-5029

Job hotline. Recorded information about current job vacancies, requirements, and instructions on how to apply.

FEDERAL CARTRIDGE

(612) 323-3863

Job hotline. Recorded message includes job descriptions, qualifications, and application procedure.

FEDERAL JOBS HOTLINE
Twin Cities Area Office

(612) 725-3430

Job hotline. Computerized job information system lists wide variety of federal job openings. This is a popular jobline. For easier access, call on weekday evenings or weekends.

FEDERAL RESERVE BANK OF MINNEAPOLIS
(612) 340-2120

Job hotline. Recorded information lists positions available, job descriptions, requirements, and application procedure.

FEDERAL WOMEN'S PROGRAM
(612) 725-3434

Job hotline. Recorded message lists federal jobs for women.

FLUOROWARE
(612) 368-8088

Job hotline. Recorded message lists current job openings, salary range, and directions on how to apply.

GENERAL MILLS
(612) 540-2334

Job hotline. Recorded message includes current job opportunities and application instructions.

GILLETTE COMPANY
(612) 292-2924

Job hotline. Recorded information includes current job vacancies and application process.

GRACO
(612) 623-6389

Job hotline. Recorded message includes job vacancies and application process. Updated weekly.

GREEN TREE FINANCIAL CORPORATION
(612) 293-5825

Job hotline. Recorded message lists job descriptions, requirements, and application process. Updated weekly.

JOB HOTLINES

HAMLINE UNIVERSITY
(612) 659-3046

Job hotline. Recorded information includes job descriptions, requirements, salary range, and application process. Updated weekly.

HEALTH RISK MANAGEMENT
(612) 829-3500 ext. 3695

Job hotline. Recorded message includes current job descriptions, requirements, and application process. Updated weekly.

HENNEPIN COUNTY
(612) 348-4698

Job hotline. Recorded message describes job openings, salary range, requirements, and application procedure for Hennepin County government jobs. Updated weekly.

HOFFMAN ENGINEERING
(612) 422-2559

Job hotline. Recorded message describes current job vacancies and application procedure.

HONEYWELL
(612) 951-2914

Job hotline. Recorded message describes current job openings, descriptions, location, requirements, and application instructions.

HUBBARD BROADCASTING (KSTP)
(612) 645-6060 Category 1919

Job hotline. Recorded message describes current job openings, salary range, requirements, and directions on how to apply.

IBM—ROCHESTER
(507) 253-8070

Job hotline. Recorded message lists current job vacancies.

IDS
(612) 671-5059

Job hotline. Recorded message lists current job descriptions, salary range, requirements, and application process.

ITT CONSUMER FINANCE
(800) 877-5627

Job hotline. Recorded message describes current job descriptions, location, requirements, and application process.

INDEPENDENT SCHOOL DISTRICT 281
(612) 533-2781

Ask for hotline. Recorded information lists current job vacancies, descriptions, and application process.

LAND O' LAKES/CENEX
(612) 481-2250

Job hotline. Recorded information includes job description, location, requirements, salary, and application procedure. Updated weekly.

LAW ENFORCEMENT AND SECURITY HOTLINE
National Association of Chiefs of Police
American Federation of Police Operators
(305) 573-0202   (800) 333-1888

Job hotline. Must be association member. Provides job descriptions, locations, salary range, requirements, and application instructions.

LIBERTY DIVERSIFIED INDUSTRIES
(612) 536-6656

Job hotline. Recorded listings for current job openings and application instructions.

JOB HOTLINES

LITTLE SIX CASINO (MYSTIC LAKE)
(612) 496-3532

Job hotline. Recorded listings include current job opportunities and application procedure.

MSI INSURANCE
(612) 639-5500

Job hotline. Recorded message includes job descriptions, requirements, and application process. Updated weekly.

MACALESTER COLLEGE
(612) 696-6400

Job hotline. Recorded information includes current job descriptions, requirements, location, and application procedure.

MARQUETTE BANK
(612) 341-5699   (612) 661-3838

Job hotline. Recorded message lists job titles, pay range, description, qualifications, and application procedure.

MARRIOTT
(612) 349-4077—City Center
(612) 854-3809—Bloomington

Job hotline. Recorded message lists current job descriptions, salary range, requirements, and application process.

MAYO FOUNDATION—ROCHESTER
(507) 284-2500

Job hotline. Call after 4 p.m. Listings include current job descriptions, location, requirements, and application process.

This chapter continues on the following page.

MCGLYNN BAKERY
(612) 574-2222

Ask for hotline. Recording describes job descriptions, locations, and application instructions.

METRO TRANSIT COMMISSION (MTC)
(612) 349-7557

Job hotline. Recorded message describes general hiring needs and application procedures for MTC.

METROPOLITAN FINANCIAL CORPORATION
(612) 928-5678

Job hotline. Recorded information includes current job descriptions, requirements, location, and application instructions.

MINNEAPOLIS CHILDREN'S MEDICAL CENTER
(612) 863-6400

Job hotline. Recorded message describes job descriptions, requirements, and application procedure. Updated weekly.

MINNEAPOLIS POST OFFICE
(612) 349-9100 message 811

Job hotline. Recorded listing of exams offered statewide by the Postal Service for new entrants.

MINNEGASCO
(612) 342-4666

Job hotline. Recorded listing of job vacancies specifying job title, description, and qualifications. Updated weekly.

MINNESOTA COMMUNITY COLLEGES
(612) 297-8261   (800) 657-3656   TDD (612) 282-2729

Job hotline. Recorded message of job openings and directions on how to apply. Updated weekly.

JOB HOTLINES

MINNESOTA MUTUAL LIFE INSURANCE
(612) 298-7934

Job hotline. Recorded message for office/technical positions. Application information is provided for professional and managerial positions.

MINNESOTA TELECOMMUNICATIONS ASSO.
(612) 671-7333

Job hotline. Recorded information includes job descriptions and application procedure.

MINNESOTA WOMEN IN THE TRADES
(612) 228-1271

Job hotline. Recorded information includes current job descriptions, locations, salary range, requirements, and directions on how to apply.

MULTIFOODS
(612) 340-3923

Job hotline. Recorded message includes current job vacancies and application procedure.

NATIONAL COMPUTER SYSTEMS
(612) 829-3005

Job hotline. Recorded information describes job descriptions, requirements, and application process. Updated weekly.

NORTHERN STATES POWER
(612) 330-6000   Tape #562

Job hotline. Recorded message provides general information on how to apply for employment. Updated bi-weekly.

NORTHWEST AIRLINES
(612) 726-3600

Job hotline. Recorded message describes hiring needs and general application procedures.

NORTHWEST HEALTH CLUB
(612) 673-1229

Job hotline. Recorded message includes job descriptions, requirements, location, and application process. Updated weekly.

NORTHWESTERN NATIONAL LIFE
(612) 342-3594

Job hotline. Recorded message includes job description, salary range, and instructions for applying. Recording states that preference is given to applications of current employees. Updated bi-weekly.

NORWEST BANK
(612) 667-JOBS

Job hotline. Recorded message lists job vacancies at numerous bank locations. Updated weekly.

PACE INC.
(612) 525-3480

Job hotline. Recorded message lists current job descriptions, requirements, and directions on how to apply.

PILLSBURY
(612) 330-4302

Job hotline. Recorded message describes general application procedures.

PIPER JAFFRAY
(612) 342-1099

Job hotline. Recorded message of job descriptions, salary range, requirements, and application procedure. Updated weekly.

JOB HOTLINES

PRUDENTIAL INSURANCE COMPANY
MINNEAPOLIS OFFICE
(612) 553-5991

Job hotline. Recorded message provides job titles, salary range, and brief description. Updated weekly.

RADISSON HOTEL SOUTH
(612) 893-8416

Job hotline. Recorded listings describe current job vacancies, salary range, and application process. Updated weekly.

RAMSEY COUNTY
(612) 266-2666

Job hotline. Recorded information includes job description, salary range, requirements and instructions for applying.

ROLLERBLADE
(612) 930-7003

Leave name and number on machine to receive information, or request employment application.

ST. PAUL POST OFFICE
(612) 293-3050

Job hotline. Recorded message includes schedule of exams offered statewide by Postal Service for new entrants.

SCIENCE MUSEUM OF MINNESOTA
(612) 221-9488

Job hotline. Recorded message includes current job descriptions, requirements, salary range, and instructions on how to apply.

This chapter continues on the following page.

SPECIAL LIBRARIES ASSOCIATION
(202) 234-3632

Job hotline. Recorded message lists job descriptions, locations, salary range, requirements, and application process. Updated bi-weekly.

ST. PAUL PIONEER PRESS
(612) 228-5008

Job hotline. Recorded message lists current positions available, job description, qualifications, salary range, and hours required.

ST. PAUL RAMSEY MEDICAL CENTER
(612) 221-4302

Job hotline. Recorded information includes current job descriptions, requirements, salary range, and application procedure.

STAR TRIBUNE
(612) 673-4075

Job hotline. Recorded listings of job vacancies. Updated bi-weekly.

STATE OF MINNESOTA
(612) 296-2616

Job hotline. Recorded information includes job description, salary range, requirements, and instructions for applying for state government jobs.

SUPERVALU
(612) 932-4777

Job hotline. Recorded message lists current job descriptions, requirements, salary range, and application procedure.

SYSCO MINNESOTA
(612) 785-7285

Job hotline. Recorded listings of current job descriptions, requirements, and application process.

JOB HOTLINES

TARGET HEADQUARTERS
(612) 335-4960

Job hotline. Recorded message with information about current job openings and application process.

TWIN CITIES PERSONNEL ASSOCIATION
(612) 832-3898

Job hotline. Recorded message describes job vacancies, locations, requirements, and application process. Updated weekly.

UNITED & CHILDREN'S HOSPITAL
(612) 220-JOBS

Job hotline. Recorded information includes job descriptions, requirements, and application process. Updated weekly.

UNITED FOR EXCELLENCE INC.
(612) 439-1561

Ask for jobline. Recording lists current job opportunities and instructions on how to apply.

UNIVERSITY OF MINNESOTA
(612) 645-6060 Category 2500

Job hotline. Recorded message describes wide variety of job opportunities with qualifications and pay range.

UNIVERSITY OF ST. THOMAS
(612) 962-6520

Job hotline. Recorded message includes job descriptions, requirements, and instructions on how to apply. Updated weekly.

VAUGHN COMMUNICATIONS
(612) 832-3260

Job hotline. Recorded message includes current job vacancies, descriptions, location, requirements, and application procedure.

WALKER ART CENTER
(612) 375-7588

Job hotline. Recorded message lists current job vacancies and directions on how to apply.

WASHINGTON COUNTY
(612) 430-6084

Job hotline. Recorded message includes description, qualifications, salary level, application procedures.

WAUSAU INSURANCE COMPANY
(612) 820-3413

Job hotline. Recorded message describes current job opportunities and instructions on how to apply.

WCCO TELEVISION
(612) 339-4444

Ask for jobline. Recorded information describes current job descriptions, requirements, and application procedure.

WILDER FOUNDATION
(612) 642-2087

Job hotline. Recorded message includes job descriptions, salary range, location, requirements, and application process. Updated weekly.

EMPLOYMENT AGENCIES & SEARCH FIRMS

Before you mail off your resume to every search firm and employment agency in the Yellow Pages, let's put to rest the confusion between these two types of organizations and what they can do for you.

Employment agencies are placement services which typically work with new college graduates or hourly personnel to help them find suitable positions. Employment agencies in Minnesota and Wisconsin are permitted to charge fees to job seekers, and employers.

Search firms (also called "headhunters" or "executive recruiters") are usually geared to seeking out candidates for highly compensated positions, $50,000 or more, and cannot charge fees to job seekers.

There are two types of search firms: retainer and contingency. A retainer firm is hired by a client company to recruit candidates for high-level positions. Retainer firms are paid whether or not they find a suitable match. A contingency firm, on the other hand, is given a "work order" by an employer and asked to fill an opening. These firms are paid only if the position is filled.

All search firms have focused assignments. They work for client employers to scour the job market for specific candidates for specific job openings. They are not in business to market job seekers to potential employers. As such, some do not welcome cold calls from candidates. A good rule of thumb is to mail your resume and follow up by phone. To contact a firm listed in this book, follow the advice they've provided on how to apply.

MINNESOTA JOB SEEKER'S SOURCEBOOK

Here are a few tips about search firms and employment agencies:

◆ Most recruitment and employment firms specialize in a particular industry or management level. Investigate which organizations specialize in your area, and contact each one.

◆ Career changers, don't look to placement services. Recruiters are primarily interested in your proven track record and industry knowledge—not in your career potential.

◆ Is the organization an employment agency or a search firm? If in doubt, Minnesota residents can call the Minnesota Department of Labor and Industry, Division of Labor Standards, (612) 296-2282; Wisconsin residents, call the Equal Rights Department, Labor Standards Division, (608) 266-3345.

◆ Does the search firm work on a contingency or retainer basis? Contingency firms may be more receptive to cold calls from job seekers, and more willing to keep your name for future opportunities.

◆ Understand your financial obligations. Employment agencies can charge you a fee; search firms cannot.

◆ For a more expansive listing of search or employment agencies, check the library reference section for the Directory of Executive Recruiters (Kennedy Publications), The Career Makers: America's Top 100 Executive Recruiters (Harper & Row), and the Directory of U.S. Search Firms (Market Advantage Group).

◆ Consider the issue of confidentiality. Will your resume be faxed throughout the industry? Clarify the firm's policies.

◆ Less than 10 percent of all job seekers use recruitment firms in their job search. Be realistic about the role these organizations may play in your overall strategy.

SEARCH FIRMS & EMPLOYMENT AGENCIES

TWIN CITIES

ACCOUNTANTS EXCHANGE, INC.
Roseville Professional Center
2233 Hamline Ave. No., Suite 509
Roseville, MN 55113
(612) 636-5490   Fax—(612) 636-8799

Search firm. Specializes in recruitment for all positions in accounting and financial fields. Mail resume; follow up by phone. Fees paid by employer.

ACCOUNTANTS EXECUTIVE SEARCH
45 So. 7th St., Suite 2312
Minneapolis, MN 55403
(612) 336-4440   Fax—(612) 341-3284

Search firm. Specializes in permanent placement of accountants, financial analysts, and other high-level positions in the financial field. Call for appointment. Fees paid by employer.

ACCOUNTANTS ON CALL
45 So. 7th St., Suite 2312
Minneapolis, MN 55402
(612) 341-9900   Fax—(612) 341-3284

Search firm. Specializes in permanent and temporary placement of accountants at all levels. Call for appointment. Fees paid by employer.

ACCOUNTANTS PLACEMENT REGISTRY
1703 Cope Avenue
Maplewood, MN 55109
(612) 773-9018   Fax—(612) 770-2633

Search firm. Specializes in accounting and finance industries. Placements for bookkeepers, accountants, accounting managers, financial analysts, executive level financial positions. Also offers contract assignments. Fees paid by employer.

This chapter continues on the following page.

MINNESOTA JOB SEEKER'S SOURCEBOOK

ADVANCE PERSONNEL RESOURCES
715 Florida Ave., Suite 410
Minneapolis, MN 55426
(612) 546-6779   Fax—(612) 541-1149

Search firm. Specializes in permanent placements of sales professionals and managers, marketing personnel, manufacturing managers, and experienced administrators. Fees paid by employer.

ADVANCED PERSONNEL PLACEMENT
2499 Rice St., Suite 206
St. Paul, MN 55113
(612) 481-9709   Fax—(612) 481-7821

Search firm. Permanent placements of experienced workers through mid-management in human resources, advertising/public relations, mortgage banking, office occupations, and customer service. Call for appointment. Fees paid by employer.

AGRI CONSULTANTS
300 So. Hwy. 169, Suite 180
Minneapolis, MN 55426
(612) 542-8550

Search firm. Specializes in agricultural sales, manufacturing product sales, research and management. Mail resume; follow up by phone. Fees paid by employer.

AGRI SEARCH
7550 France Ave. So., Suite 180
Minneapolis, MN 55435
(612) 830-1569   Fax—(612) 893-9254

Search firm. Specializes in placement of sales, management, and technical personnel in the agriculture industry. Call for appointment. Fees paid by employer.

SEARCH FIRMS & EMPLOYMENT AGENCIES

AGRO QUALITY SEARCH INC.
7260 University Ave. N.E., Suite 305
Minneapolis, MN 55432
(612) 572-3737

Search firm. Placement of personnel in management, sales, marketing, technical, production, and service areas of the agriculture/food industries. Mail resume; follow up by phone. Fees paid by employer.

ALTERNATIVE STAFFING, INC.
8120 Penn Ave. So., Suite 570
Bloomington, MN 55431
(612) 888-6077   Fax—(612) 888-6153

Search firm. Specializes in permanent and temporary placement of office support, accounting, and mortgage personnel. Call for appointment. Fees paid by employer.

BRIGHT SEARCH / PROFESSIONAL STAFFING
8120 Penn Ave. So.
Minneapolis, MN 55431
(612) 884-8111

Search firm. Recruits and markets mid-level professionals in sales, marketing, engineering, and technical specialties. Nationwide coverage with associate agencies. Mail resume and salary requirements. Fees paid by employer.

CAREER CENTERS, INC.
7300 France Ave. So., Suite 210
Edina, MN 55435
(612) 835-7771

Search firm. Specializes in the recruitment of experienced sales personnel. Call for appointment. Fees paid by employer.

This chapter continues on the following page.

COMPU-SEARCH INC.
7625 Metro Blvd., Suite 350
Minneapolis, MN 55439
(612) 835-0848   Fax—(612) 835-0675

Search firm. Division of nationwide company. Specializes in placement of technical and mid-management personnel in data processing. Call for appointment. Fees paid by employer.

COMPUTER PERSONNEL R PARTNERS
5353 Wayzata Blvd., Suite 604
Minneapolis, MN 55416
(612) 542-8053

Search firm. Permanent placement for mid- to upper management positions in the computer industry. Call for appointment. Fees paid by employer.

CORPORATE RESOURCES PROFESSIONAL PLACEMENT
4205 Lancaster Lane, #108
Plymouth, MN 55441
(612) 550-9222   Fax—(612) 550-9657

Search firm. Permanent placement of all levels in the agricultural, mechanical, electrical, software engineering, and biomedical industries. Fax or mail resume; follow-up by phone. Fees paid by employer.

ELLS PERSONNEL
9900 Bren Road E., Suite 105
Minneapolis, MN 55343
(612) 932-9933   Fax—(612) 932-0099

Search firm. Specializes in placement of middle and senior level management in banking, building products, printing, engineering and sales. Also offers contract employment. Mail resume; follow up by phone. Fees paid by employer.

SEARCH FIRMS & EMPLOYMENT AGENCIES

ESP SYSTEMS PROFESSIONALS, INC.
701 Fourth Ave. So., Suite 1800
Minneapolis, MN 55415
(612) 337-3000   Fax—(612) 337-9199

Search firm. Specializes in data processing industry. Positions include programmers, systems analysts, project leaders, managers, systems programmers, programmer analysts. Mail resume; follow up by phone. Fees paid by employer.

ESQUIRE SEARCH LTD.
430 First Ave. No., Suite 630
Minneapolis, MN 55401
(612) 340-9068   Fax—(612) 340-1218

Search firm. Specializes in permanent placement of all levels of attorneys, paralegals, and legal assistants. Call for appointment. Fees paid by employer.

EXECU-TECH SEARCH, INC.
3600 W. 80th Street
Bloomington, MN 55431
(612) 893-6915   Fax—(612) 896-3479

Search firm. Specializes in permanent placement of design engineers through upper management within the food, beverage, and chemical industry and architectural engineering firms. Fax resume; follow up by phone. Fees paid by employer.

H R SERVICES
3030 Harbor Lane, Suite 200-F
Plymouth, MN 55447
(612) 559-8841

Search firm. Specializes in placement of personnel with two years experience through upper management positions in the engineering, industrial, and technical manufacturing industries. Mail resume; follow-up by phone. Fees paid by employer.

This chapter continues on the following page.

MINNESOTA JOB SEEKER'S SOURCEBOOK

HEALTHCARE RECRUITERS OF MINNESOTA
6458 City West Parkway, Suite 100
Eden Prairie, MN 55344
(612) 943-3940   Fax—(612) 340-9518

Search firm. National healthcare recruiter. Placement of executive level management, sales, marketing, and technical personnel in medical field; nurses at management level, and physicians. Mail resume; follow up by phone. Fees paid by employer.

HENNEPIN COUNTY BAR ASSOCIATION PLACEMENT SERVICE
514 Nicollet Mall, Suite 350
Minneapolis, MN 55402
(612) 340-0022

Search firm. Specializes in part-time, full-time and temporary placement of support staff in the legal profession. Call for appointment. Fees paid by employer.

INSURANCE TALENT / BUSINESS TALENT
P.O. Box 40064
St. Paul, MN 55104
(612) 690-0695   Fax—(612) 699-7031

Search firm. Specializes in recruitment of sales, underwriting and loss control professionals in the property and casualty insurance industry; and retained search for sales, marketing, customer service, management, and technical positions in diverse industries. Mail resume; follow up by phone. Fees paid by employer.

KORN/FERRY INTERNATIONAL
4816 IDS Center
Minneapolis, MN 55402
(612) 333-1834   Fax—(612) 333-8971

Search firm. Local general practice office of international recruiting firm. Recruitment of executive-level management only. Mail resume and cover letter. Fees paid by employer.

SEARCH FIRMS & EMPLOYMENT AGENCIES

KREOFSKY AND ASSOCIATES
8400 Normandale Lake Blvd., Suite 934
Bloomington, MN 55437
(612) 921-8820

Search firm. Specializes in computer sales and technical pre-sales personnel. Mail resume; follow up by phone. Fees paid by employer.

KULLER-FLEMING AND ASSOCIATES
4121 Randall Avenue
St. Louis Park, MN 55416
(612) 926-3375   Fax—(612) 928-0511

Search firm. Specializes in executive level management in medical manufacturing. Mail resume; follow up by phone. Fees paid by employer.

LEE MARSH AND ASSOCIATES
202 No. One Appletree Square
Bloomington, MN 55425
(612) 854-6811   Fax—(612) 452-9051

Search firm. Permanent placement of experienced workers through mid-management in the software engineering industry. Fax resume; follow up by phone. Fees paid by employer.

MANAGEMENT RECRUITERS
7625 Metro Blvd.
Minneapolis, MN 55439
(612) 835-4466   Fax—(612) 835-0675

Search firm. Recruitment of administrative, technical, sales/marketing professionals for diverse industries. Affiliated with 400 offices nationwide. Call for appointment. Fees paid by employer.

MARY ERICKSON & ASSOCIATES
8300 Norman Center Drive, Suite 545
Minneapolis, MN 55437
(612) 893-1010   Fax—(612) 893-0130

Search firm. Industry generalist. Specializes in executive search only at senior level. Mail resume; follow up by phone. Fees paid by employer.

MASTERSON PERSONNEL INC.
5775 Wayzata Blvd., Suite 995
St. Louis Park, MN 55416
(612) 542-9300   Fax—(612) 542-3143

Search firm. Permanent, temporary, and contract placement of entry level positions in data processing, computer operator, and other office services. Call for appointment. Fees paid by employer.

MEDSEARCH CORP.
Southdale Medical Center
6545 France Ave. So.
Edina, MN 55435
(612) 926-6584   Fax—(612) 926-7584

Employment agency. Placement in all areas of medical field including support staff, executives, physicians. Mail resume; follow up by phone. Generally, fees paid by employer.

PFAFFLY PERSONNEL RESOURCES
3055 Old Hwy. 8
Minneapolis, MN 55418
(612) 782-2445   Fax—(612) 782-2318

Employment agency. Permanent and some temporary placement of experienced medical personnel through upper level management. Call for appointment. Fees paid by employer.

PINNACLE SEARCH LTD.
2500 W. County Road 42
Burnsville, MN 55337
(612) 894-7700

Search firm and employment agency. Specializes in permanent placement of mid-management positions in the paper, printing, and packaging industries. Call for appointment. Fees paid by employer.

SEARCH FIRMS & EMPLOYMENT AGENCIES

ROBERT HALF INTERNATIONAL INC.
Call for locations in Bloomington, Plymouth and St. Paul.
2800 Norwest Center, 90 So. 7th Street
Minneapolis, MN 55402
(612) 339-9001

Search firm. Recruitment of financial execs, accountants, bookkeepers, information systems professionals. Mail resume; follow up by phone.

ROTH YOUNG EXECUTIVE RECRUITERS
4530 W. 77th St., Suite 250
Minneapolis, MN 55435
(612) 831-6655   Fax—(612) 831-7413

Search firm. Recruitment of mid/senior management in hotel and restaurant industries, food manufacturing, sales, retailing, supermarket and food wholesalers, and health care. Mail resume; follow up by phone.

SALES CONSULTANTS OF MINNEAPOLIS
7550 France Ave., Suite 180
Minneapolis, MN 55435
(612) 830-1420   Fax—(612) 893-9254

Search firm. Recruits for sales, sales management, and marketing personnel. Call for appointment. Fees paid by employer.

SATHE & ASSOCIATES
5821 Cedar Lake Road
Minneapolis, MN 55416
(612) 546-2100   Fax—(612) 546-6930

Retainer search firm. Industry generalists with emphasis in senior management. Mail resume and cover letter. Fees paid by employer.

SNELLING AND SNELLING
2665 Long Lake Rd., Suite 220
Roseville, MN 55113
(612) 631-3040   Fax—(612) 631-1455

Search firm. Placement of mid-management accounting and finance personnel. Mail resume; follow up by phone. Fees paid by employer.

SOURCE SERVICES
8400 Normandale Lake Blvd., Suite 1430
Bloomington, MN 55437
(612) 835-5100   Fax—(612) 835-1548

Search firm. Permanent and contract positions for experienced personnel in computers, finance, and accounting. Call for appointment. Fees paid by employer.

T.H. HUNTER, INC.
526 Nicollet Mall, Suite 310
Minneapolis, MN 55402
(612) 339-0530   Fax—(612) 338-4757

Search firm. Generalists with emphasis in banking, engineering, data processing, marketing, medical, finance and insurance. Most positions are middle management; some at senior level. Call for appointment. Fees paid by employer.

THE MAZZITELLI GROUP LTD.
603 E. Lake St., Suite 200-K
Wayzata, MN 55391
(612) 449-9490

Search firm. Executive search practice specializing in the permanent placement of executive and senior management positions nationwide. Mail resume and cover letter. Fees paid by employer.

THE RECRUITING GROUP
5354 Parkdale Dr., Suite 104
Minneapolis, MN 55416
(612) 544-8550   Fax—(612) 546-2806

Search firm. Permanent and temporary placement of mid to upper-management positions in various industries. Fax or mail resume; follow-up by phone. Fees paid by employer.

SEARCH FIRMS & EMPLOYMENT AGENCIES

WHITNEY & ASSOCIATES, INC.
920 Second Ave. So., Suite 625
Minneapolis, MN 55402-4035
(612) 338-5600   Fax—(612) 349-6129

Search firm. Specializes in staff and management personnel in accounting and finance fields. Mail resume. Fees paid by employer.

NORTHERN MINNESOTA

AAA EMPLOYMENT AGENCY OF DULUTH
2631 W. Superior Street
Duluth, MN 55806
(218) 727-8810   Fax—(218) 727-8830

Employment agency. Permanent placement of all levels in all non-government types of positions. Call for appointment. Fees paid upon placement by job seeker.

MCGLADREY AND PULLEN
700 Missabe Bldg.
Duluth, MN 55802
(218) 727-5025   Fax—(218) 727-1438

Search firm. Permanent placements of upper and mid-management positions in diverse industries. Also provides outplacement services. Call for appointment. Fees paid by employer.

OLSTEN'S STAFFING SERVICE
110 Fitger Complex
600 E. Superior Street
Duluth, MN 55812
(218) 720-3265   Fax—(218) 720-3325

Search firm. Permanent and temporary positions in diverse industries. Call for appointment. Fees paid by employer.

This chapter continues on the following page.

CENTRAL MINNESOTA

DELACORE RESOURCES
101 Park Place, Suite 206
Hutchinson, MN 55350
(612) 587-4420   Fax—(612) 587-7252

Search firm. Specializes in permanent placements of healthcare positions including physicians, CRNAs, physical therapists, and staff. Call or mail resume. Fee paid by employer.

NORTH STAR EMPLOYMENT
3700 W. Division Street
St. Cloud, MN 56301
(612) 252-3522

Employment agency. Permanent placement in all occupational areas from entry level through executive. Fees are paid by the employer and/or the applicant. Call for an appointment or mail resume.

SOUTHERN MINNESOTA

EXPRESS PERSONNEL SERVICES
2360 No. Broadway
Rochester, MN 55906
(507) 285-9224

1380 W. Main
Albert Lea, MN 56007
(507) 373-2826   (800) 898-2826

812 So. Elm
Owatonna, MN 55060
(507) 455-3002   (800) 832-3002

Employment agency. Specializes in temporary and permanent placements for entry-level, clerical and office support staff. Call for appointment. Fees paid by applicant.

SEARCH FIRMS & EMPLOYMENT AGENCIES

LEIDERS EMPLOYMENT SERVICE
210 First Ave. SW, Suite 429
Rochester, MN 55902
(507) 285-1425   Fax—(507) 285-1428

Employment agency. Professional career placements at all levels in diverse industries. Permanent and temporary positions. Call for appointment. Fees may be paid by employer or by applicant.

MANAGEMENT RECRUITERS OF ROCHESTER
1903 So. Broadway
Rochester, MN 55904
(507) 282-2400   Fax—(507) 282-1308

Search firm. Specializes in permanent and temporary executive positions for information systems personnel, professionals and healthcare specialists. Fax or mail resume, or call for appointment. Fees paid by employer.

RWJ AND ASSOCIATES
2360 No. Broadway
Rochester, MN 55906
(507) 285-9270   Fax—(507) 285-1830

Search firm. Specializes in permanent positions for mid- to upper management for industry generalists. Mail resume; follow up by phone. Fees paid by employer.

TECHNICAL CAREER PLACEMENTS INC.
1915 Highway 52 No., Suite 222-C
Rochester, MN 55901
(507) 288-3623   Fax—(507) 288-6586

Search firm. Permanent and contract placements of mid- to upper managers in engineering; hardware/software engineers; and computer programmers. Mail or fax resume; call for appointment. Generally fees paid by employer.

This chapter continues on the following page.

WESTERN WISCONSIN

CAREER RESOURCES / STAFFING RESOURCES
757 Sand Lake Road
Onalaska, WI 54650
(608) 783-6307   Fax—(608) 783-6302

Search firm. Permanent and contract positions for upper and mid management, M.I.S., human resources, accounting. Mail resume; follow up by phone for initial screening. Fees paid by employer.

EMPLOYMENT SPECIALISTS
421 Main St., Suite 207
La Crosse, WI 54601
(608) 791-1111   Fax—(608) 791-1113

Search firm. Specializes in recruitment of engineers, technical tool makers, and operations managers in plastics manufacturing industry. Call for appointment. Fees paid by employer.

PERSONNEL UNLIMITED EXECUTIVE SEARCH
1285 Rudy St., Suite 101-A
Onalaska, WI 54650
(608) 781-7250

Search firm. Recruitment of sales and marketing management positions primarily in medical field. Mail resume; follow up by phone. Fees paid by employer.

PROFESSIONAL BUSINESS SERVICES
P.O. Box 1392
Eau Claire, WI 54702
715/836-9949   Fax—715/836-9871

Search firm. Permanent, and some temporary, placements at manufacturers in northern Wisconsin. Positions primarily in engineering, but may include general management, marketing, sales, M.I.S., human resources, accounting. Call or send resume. Fees paid by employer.

RECRUITMENT PUBLICATIONS

If you're intent on tracking down current job leads, don't overlook recruitment publications. These interesting "positions available" periodicals range from chatty newsletters to slick, career-track magazines. One may be just the ticket to your next job.

Recruitment publications have a diverse appeal. Many cater to general employment markets; others are tightly focused on jobs within specific industries or professions. Still others report job vacancies by type of employer (federal government, non-profit organizations) or by the job seeker's level of experience (senior management, new college graduates).

There's also a variation in the content between recruitment publications. Many offer nothing more than a straightforward listing of job openings; others provide an interesting selection of "how-to" articles and job-seeking tips.

Only a handful of recruitment publications exclusively list Minnesota and Wisconsin job vacancies. It's more common to find publications with a nationwide circulation that list job openings throughout the country.

Look for only a small number of recruitment publications at area newsstands. The majority are available only by subscription. Although subscriptions are generally short-term, it's a good idea to request a sample copy before subscribing.

AFFIRMATIVE ACTION REGISTER
8356 Olive Blvd.
St. Louis, MO 63132
(800) 537-0655   Fax—(314) 997-1788

Free monthly publication directed to females, minorities, veterans, and the handicapped. Each issue includes approximately 150 job vacancies at colleges, universities, government, hospitals, and other organizations nationwide. Most positions are managerial and professional. Call to be added to the mailing list.

AIR JOBS DIGEST
5640 Nicholson Lane, Suite 203
Rockville, MD 20852
(800) AIR-JOBS   Fax—(301) 984-4188

Monthly tabloid with 500—1,000 worldwide job opportunities in aviation, aerospace, and space industries. Positions for pilots, mechanics, technicians, flight attendants, engineers, management. Subscription, $39/3 issues; $59/6 issues.

ARTJOB
236 Montezuma Avenue
Santa Fe, NM 87501
(505) 988-1166   Fax—(505) 982-9307

Bi-weekly newsletter with 100 art opportunities with agencies, presenting organizations, academic institutions. Subscription, $30/12 issues; $45/24 issues. Sample issue on request.

ATHLETIC EMPLOYMENT WEEKLY
Route 2, Box 140
Carthage, IL 62321
(217) 357-3615

Weekly newsletter listing 75—200 coaching and athletic positions in two- and four-year colleges throughout the U.S. Subscription rates, $40/24 issues; $65/48 issues. Call or write for free sample issue.

RECRUITMENT PUBLICATIONS

CAREER CONNECTIONS
P.O. Box 10129
Phoenix, AZ 85064
(800) 776-7877   Fax—(602) 955-3441

Bi-weekly newsletter with approximately 50 job opportunities nationwide in the business aspect of the sports industry. Subscription rate, $100/12 issues.

COMMUNITY JOBS
50 Beacon Street
Boston, MA 02108
(617) 720-5627   Fax—(617) 720-1318

Monthly tabloid with editorial articles and 220—250 job vacancies, entry-level through senior executive, at non-profit organizations throughout the U.S. Subscription, $25/three months; $39/six months. Call or write for information.

CONTRACT EMPLOYMENT WEEKLY
P.O. Box 97000
Kirkland, WA 98083-9700
(206) 823-2222   Fax—(206) 821-0942

Weekly newsletter. Each issue includes approximately 3,000—4,000 contract technical job opportunities, nationwide and overseas. Call or write for information. Subscription rate, $30/15 issues. A free sample is available on request.

CURRENT JOBS FOR GRADUATES
P.O. Box 3505
McLean, Virginia 22103
(703) 506-4400

National employment bulletin for liberal arts professions. Published twice monthly. Each issue lists approximately 200—250 job vacancies throughout the U.S. for entry level or early career positions. Subscription, $25/6 issues; $59/24 issues. Call or write to subscribe.

MINNESOTA JOB SEEKER'S SOURCEBOOK

EMPLOYMENT REVIEW
1655 Palm Beach Lakes Blvd., Suite 600
West Palm Beach, FL 33401
(407) 686-6800   Fax—(407) 686-8340

Monthly nationwide tabloid with job listings focused predominantly in finance and high-tech. Editorial support articles. Approximately 75 listings in 60 pages. Available at local newsstands. Subscription, $10.95/6 issues; $19.95/12 issues. Call or write for information.

ENVIRONMENTAL CAREER OPPORTUNITIES
P.O. Box 15629
Chevy Chase, MD 20825
(301) 986-5545   Fax—(301) 986-0658

Bi-weekly magazine with 300 national job opportunities in the public and private sector of environmental field. Subscription, $29/4 issues; $49/8 issues. Sample on request.

ENVIRONMENTAL OPPORTUNITIES
P.O. Box 788
Walpole, NH 03608
(603) 756-4553

Monthly newsletter with listings for entry- to mid-level jobs, nationwide, in the environmental field. Experience requirements range from 0-10 years. Includes seasonal positions and internships. Call or write for free sample. Subscription, $26/6 issues; $47/12 issues.

EXEC-U-NET
25 Van Zant St., Suite 15-3
Norwalk, CT 06855
(203) 851-5180   (800) 637-3126

Bi-weekly newsletter for senior level executives with incomes over $70,000. Approximately 175 positions per issue in general management, finance, sales, marketing, operations management in all industries. Must join executive network designed to assist in active career management. Membership, $260/year; $150/6 months; $95/3 months. Call for information and member services.

RECRUITMENT PUBLICATIONS

FEDERAL CAREER OPPORTUNITIES
P.O. Box 1059
Vienna, VA 22183-1059
(800) 822-JOBS   Fax—(703) 281-7639

Bi-weekly. Each issue lists 4,000 job openings at all agencies of federal government from GS-5 level to senior executive level. Subscription, $38/6 issues; $75/12 issues. Also available on-line, $45/hour. Write or call to subscribe.

FEDERAL JOBS DIGEST
325 Pennsylvania Avenue S.E.
Washington, DC 20003
(800) 824-5000   Fax—(914) 762-5695

Bi-weekly tabloid lists federal job openings nationwide. Editions for individuals looking for first federal job and for current federal employees. Also offers Federal Job Matching Service at additional fee, matching applicants to suitable federal careers. Call or write to subscribe. $29/6 issues.

INTERNATIONAL CAREER EMPLOYMENT OPPORTUNITIES
Route 2, Box 305
Stanardsville, VA 22973
(804) 985-6444   Fax—(804) 985-6828

Bi-weekly magazine listing 600—700 nationwide and overseas job opportunities in foreign policy, education, communication, trade and finance, environmental programs, development and assistance, health care. Subscription, $29/4 issues; $49/8 issues. Free issue upon request.

INTERNATIONAL EMPLOYMENT GAZETTE
1525 Wade Hampton Blvd.
Greenville, SC 29609
(800) 882-9188   Fax—(803) 235-3369

Bi-weekly 64-page magazine with over 400 overseas job opportunities. Primarily white-collar positions. Call for informational brochure. Available at selected local bookstores. Subscription, $35/6 issues.

MINNESOTA JOB SEEKER'S SOURCEBOOK

J.O.B.
Job Opportunities Bulletin For Minorities and Women In Local Government

777 No. Capitol St. N.E., Suite 500
Washington D.C. 20002
(202) 962-3662   Fax—(202) 962-3500

Bi-weekly newsletter with 25 national and international job opportunities in local and regional government professions. Subscription, $12/24 issues. Sample issue upon request.

JOB INFORMATION LETTER
National Association of Government Communicators

669 South Washington Street
Alexandria, VA 22314
(703) 519-3902   Fax—(703) 519-7732

Bi-weekly newsletter with approximately 500 communications positions with federal government and non-government employers in U.S. Free to members; $50 per year/non-members. Call or write for sample.

MINNESOTA CAREER OPPORTUNITIES
Minnesota Department of Employee Relations

200 C.O.B., 658 Cedar Street
St. Paul, MN 55155
(612) 296-2616

Bi-weekly pamphlet. Published by State of Minnesota. Lists 20—25 civil service jobs. Call for recorded instructions on how to receive publication.

NATIONAL AND FEDERAL LEGAL EMPLOYMENT REPORT

1010 Vermont Ave. N.W., Suite 408
Washington D.C. 20005
(202) 393-3311   Fax—(202) 393-1553

Monthly newsletter listing 500—600 job opportunities in the law and law-related professions throughout the U.S. and abroad. Subscription, $34/3 issues; $58/6 issues.

RECRUITMENT PUBLICATIONS

NATIONAL BUSINESS EMPLOYMENT WEEKLY
420 Lexington Avenue
New York, NY 10170
(800) 562-4868 (JOB HUNT)   Fax—(609) 520-4309

Weekly tabloid, published by Wall Street Journal, includes display ads for wide variety of job openings throughout the U.S., plus articles on job-search strategy. Bi-monthly special sections feature franchise opportunities. Available at local newsstands. Subscription, $3.95/single issue; $35/8 issues.

NATIONWIDE JOBS IN DIETETICS
P.O. Box 3537
Santa Monica, CA 90408-3537
(310) 453-5375

Bi-weekly newsletter with 450 nationwide job opportunities for dietitians, nutritionists, food service professionals. Subscription, $24/2 issues; $36/4 issues. Free sample issue on request.

PUBLIC SECTOR JOB BULLETIN
P.O. Box 1222
Newton, Iowa 50208-1222
(515) 791-9019   Fax—(515) 791-1005

Bi-weekly publication includes current job opportunities in local and state government. Subscription rate, $12/13 issues; $19/26 issues. A free sample is available on request.

SOCIAL SERVICE JOBS
10 Angelica Drive
Framingham, MA 01701
(508) 626-8644   Fax—(508) 626-9389

Bi-weekly newsletter with listings for approximately 150—170 current employment opportunities in the social services, nationwide. Subscription rate, $42/6 issues; $59/12 issues. A free sample issue is available upon request.

MINNESOTA JOB SEEKER'S SOURCEBOOK

TECHNICAL EMPLOYMENT
12416 Hymeadow Drive
Austin, TX 78750-1896
(800) 678-9724   (512) 250-8127   Fax—(512) 331-3900

Weekly magazine with over 200 job opportunities in contract technical employment. Subscription, $30/15 issues. Free sample on request.

THE JOB SEEKER
Route 2, Box 16
Warrens, WI 54666
(608) 378-4290   (608) 378-4290

Bi-weekly newsletter covers natural resources and environmental fields nationwide with 200 job vacancies per issue. Entry- through senior executive levels. Subscription, $19.50/6 issues. Call for sample.

THE NATIONAL AD SEARCH
P.O. Box 2083
Milwaukee, WI 53201
(800) 992-2832   Fax—(414) 351-0836

Weekly tabloid lists 2400 nationwide job openings by career category, compiled from 75 major Sunday newspapers. Offers resume exchange service. Subscriptions start at $40/6 issues. Free sample on request.

THE POSITION REPORT
809 Ridge Road, Suite M
Wilmette, IL 60091
(708) 256-8826   Fax—(708) 256-8937

Weekly newsletter with over 500 nationwide job opportunities in the law professions. Subscription, $43.50/4 issues.

TWIN CITIES EMPLOYMENT WEEKLY
5500 Wayzata Blvd., Suite 800
Minneapolis, MN 55416
(612) 591-2682   Fax—(612) 591-0044

Weekly tabloid with 50 current job openings. Free at metro locations.

JOB LEAD SERVICES

Job Banks & Resume Referral Services

Like any bank where deposits and withdrawals are made, a job bank is where employers "deposit" their job openings for job seekers to review. Conversely, a resume referral service is where job seekers deposit their resumes for employers to review. These services are two sides of the same coin. The goal is to bring employers and job hunters together, to hire and be hired.

Job banks generally require an active role by the job seeker. To use a job bank, the individual looking for work must browse through job listings, identify prospects, and contact employers directly. Many job banks are computer databases, some accessible by a home computer with a modem and compatible communications software.

Resume referral services, on the other hand, are passive. The only action required is to submit a clean, readable resume, or "profile" application. Some services collect and file resumes for would-be employers to examine; others actively review and match them to job descriptions submitted by employers.

Some organizations charge a fee. If you choose to work with a fee-based service, understand what you will get for your money. Ask questions like: What kind of job listings are available and from what sources? Are these listings picked up from the Sunday classified ads of metro newspapers, or from the Job Service Job Bank (which is free and open to the public)? Are listings current? Which employers have access to your resume? What kind of results can you expect?

See also Chapter Five, Networking Organizations. Many local trade and professional associations also provide job lead services.

AACC/APS JOB PLACEMENT SERVICE
American Association of Cereal Chemists
American Phytopathological Association

3340 Pilot Knob Road
St. Paul, MN 55121
(612) 454-7250   Fax—(612) 454-0766

On-line computer job bank. Open to the public. AACC is targeted to cereal science professionals; APS is targeted to plant sciences professionals. Database of 200 positions, updated weekly. Requires computer modem and communications software. Call or write for access information and fees.

ACCESS
Federal Career Opportunities On-Line

243 Church St. N.W.
Vienna, VA 22180
(703) 281-0200—Voice
(703) 281-0200—Access

On-line computer job bank. Database of 3000—4000 federal jobs, nationwide and overseas. All occupations and salary levels represented. Updated daily. Requires IBM-compatible PC and Hayes compatible modem. Set-up fee, $25. Usage charge, $45/hour. Call or write for information.

ARMY EMPLOYER NETWORK

Room 450
331 Second Ave. So.
Minneapolis, MN 55401-2253
(612) 339-3914

Computer network. Provides job leads to downsized Army personnel via database of employers in Minnesota and western Wisconsin who are interested in hiring military alumni. Call for information. Free.

JOB LEAD SERVICES

CAREER PLACEMENT REGISTRY, INC.
3202 Kirkwood Highway
Wilmington, DE 19808
(800) 331-4955

On-line resume referral service. Experienced personnel and college grads can file resumes in this computer database, available to up to 155,000 employers nationwide through DIALOG Information Services. Resumes remain in system six months. Fees for students/recent grads, $15; All others, fees start at $25. Write or call for Data Entry Form.

CENTER FOR CAREER CHANGE RESUME SERVICE
Division of Metropolitan Senior Federation
1885 University Avenue
St. Paul, MN 55104
(612) 645-0261

Resume referral service. Matches older workers, ages 55 and up, by skills and experience to listed job openings. Call for information. No charge to be listed.

JOB BANK USA
1420 Spring Hill Road, Suite 480
McLean, VA 22102
(800) 296-1872

Resume referral service. Open to the public. Serving all professions, crafts, and trades nationwide. Resumes remain on file one year, accessible to prospective employers. Call to enroll, $75.

JOB PLACEMENT
American Purchasing Society
11910 Oak Trail Way
Port Richey, FL 34668
(813) 862-7998   Fax—(813) 862-8199

Resume referral service. Targeted to purchasing/materials management, nationwide. Open to public, but members receive priority. Resumes filed for one year. Call or write for application. Annual membership, $115.

JOB EXCHANGE INC.
5270 W. 84th St., Suite 140
Bloomington, MN 55437
(612) 832-9957   Fax—(612) 832-9956

Job bank. Approximately 300-400 jobs in database for entry-level and experienced personnel in health care, retail, clerical, construction, social work, etc. Also offers resume assistance. Fees: $110 for two-month access. Call for appointment.

JOB SERVICE JOB BANK
State Department of Jobs and Training

Computer job bank. Job seekers have access to computerized data bank with many types of job openings. See Chapter Two for government Job Service locations. Free.

KINEXUS
640 North LaSalle St., Suite 560
Chicago, IL 60610
(800) 828-0422   Fax—(312) 642-0616

Resume referral service. Targeted to entry-level through experienced candidates. Resumes are broadcast to employers nationwide. Call for application. Resumes kept in system one year. Fee: $30.

NCMA JOB REFERRAL SERVICE
National Contract Managers Association
1912 Woodford Road
Vienna, VA 22182
(800) 344-8096   Fax—(703) 448-0939

Resume referral service. Targeted to individuals in contracting. Call for application. Resumes remain in system six months. Service is free to members; $70, non-members.

JOB LEAD SERVICES

ONLINE CAREER CENTER, INC.
3125 Dandy Trail
Indianapolis, IN 46214
(317) 293-6499   Fax—(317) 6692

On-line computer job bank and resume referral service. Approximately 8,000 international and domestic jobs in database, updated hourly. Resumes may also be sent on-line, and remain in system for 90 days. Call or send self-addressed, stamped envelope for access information and fees.

RESUME-ON-FILE
Association Trends Magazine
7910 Woodmont Ave., Suite 1150
Bethesda, MD 20814
(301) 652-8666   Fax—(301) 656-8654

Resume referral service. Targeted to entry-level through senior executives seeking employment in associations nationwide.

THE NEW PROFESSIONAL GROUP
P.O. Box 2007
Amherst, MA 01004-2007
(413) 549-7440—Phone
(413) 549-8136—Bulletin Board
(413) 549-7542—Fax

On-line computer job bank serving professionals in software and information systems. Approximately 1,000 nationwide job vacancies in database, updated weekly. Requires PC and modem up to 14,400. Call or write for information. Free.

This chapter continues on the following page.

TIES
Technology Information Educational Services
1925 W. County Road B2
Roseville, MN 55113
(612) 638-2339   Fax—(612) 631-7519

On-line search service. Targeted to educational professionals including teachers and administrators. Applicant's profile is matched to the hiring needs of participating employers and school districts. Call for information and fees.

TWIN CITIES COMPUTER NETWORK
60 So. Sixth St., Suite 2300
Minneapolis, MN 55402
(612) 349-6200

On-line computer job bank. Open to the public. Local employment opportunities are broadcast through this E-Mail system. Call for user information. Access is free.

CHAPTER FIVE

5

FOR NETWORKING & SUPPORT

Job hunting is a social process. And this chapter is your "people" connection. Don't go through your job hunt alone. There are more resources than you think to help you stay afloat and connected to the community during this transition.

Job support groups and networking organizations are prime places to expand your contacts, learn new skills, and feel good about who you are and what you have to offer.

If you are experiencing personal or household difficulties, there are services to reach out and give you a hand. Crisis and referral helplines offer immediate leads to community support services. Other transition services can help you sort out emotional, financial legal, and other concerns about basic living so you can take positive steps to put your life in order.

JOB SUPPORT GROUPS

Here's a bit of advice we hope you'll take: *Get thee to a job support group.*

Job support groups can provide greatly needed emotional support to job seekers. They also can offer practical no-cost job-search information, provided by career transition experts invited as guest speakers.

Most job support groups are free and open to the public, held at local churches and synagogues on a drop-in basis. At regular meetings, participants gather to support each other through the job transition process. Participants share job-search strategies, status reports of weekly progress, and support each other in dealing with the emotional and financial challenges connected with losing a job.

Twin Cities groups usually attract 10—35 people per meeting, although some like Colonial Church of Edina, and First Evangelical Lutheran Church in White Bear Lake frequently attract 75 or more. Some groups also invite spouses and partners. Though reservations are rarely required, it's a good idea to contact the sponsoring organization prior to attending to confirm the meeting schedule.

To no avail, we tried to track down job support groups operating in greater Minnesota and western Wisconsin. If your community would like to start a group, a good resource is Jobs in Transition 'N Support Group, Inc., a non-profit corporation that assists in establishing new job support groups statewide. Call or write for information: (612) 429-9594, 2150 Third Street, White Bear Lake, MN 55110.

JOB SUPPORT GROUPS

BETH EL SYNAGOGUE
Job Support Group

5224 West 26th Street
St. Louis Park, MN 55416
(612) 920-3512

Open to the public. Meets first and third Thursdays of the month, 7:30—9 p.m. Facilitated by career professionals. Meetings include presentations and group discussions. Drop in. No charge.

CALVARY LUTHERAN CHURCH
Career Change Support Group

7520 Golden Valley Road, Rm 105
Golden Valley, MN 55427
(612) 545-5659

Open to the public. Meets two Mondays per month, September through December; January through May, at 7:30 p.m. Speakers on job loss, job seeking, career alternatives. Group discussions for problem solving and support. Attracts 20—30 participants. No charge.

CENACLE RETREAT HOUSE
Retreat for the Unemployed

1221 Wayzata Blvd.
Wayzata, MN 55391
(612) 473-7308

The Cenacle offers weekend retreats for the unemployed and spouses to focus on maintaining faith, courage, and morale. Retreats held Sept. and January. Open to the public. Call for reservations. No charge.

CENTENNIAL UNITED METHODIST CHURCH
Job Transition Support Group

1524 West County Road C-2
Roseville, MN 55113
(612) 633-7644

Open to the public. Offers support and job seeking assistance at weekly meetings. Call for information and schedule. No charge.

CENTRAL LUTHERAN CHURCH
Jobs in Transition 'n Support Group

1103 School Street
Elk River, MN 55330
(612) 441-2363

Newly forming group, open to the public, plans to offer speakers, group discussions, emotional support, and networking opportunities. Call for information and schedule. No charge.

CHRIST PRESBYTERIAN CHURCH
Job Transition Support Group

6901 Normandale Road
Edina, MN 55435
(612) 920-8515

Meets Saturdays at 8:30 a.m. Focuses on emotional and spiritual needs of participants. Discussions and presentations on job-search strategies, emotional conflicts, stages of grief due to job loss. Drop in. No charge.

CHRIST THE KING CHURCH

1900 7th St. N.W.
New Brighton, MN 55112
(612) 633-4674

Support group not currently in operation, but may re-activate in future. Church provides job-search resource notebook, on loan to interested individuals. Call for information. No charge.

COLONIAL CHURCH OF EDINA
Job Transition Support Group

6200 Colonial Way
Edina, MN 55436
(612) 925-2711

Meets Mondays at 7 p.m. Attracts 75—100 participants. Guest speakers, first and third Mondays, on topics like personal marketing, employment alternatives, coping with job loss. On alternate Mondays, discussions are facilitated by volunteers. Drop in. No charge.

JOB SUPPORT GROUPS

CRYSTAL EVANGELICAL FREE CHURCH
Career Net
4225 Gettysburg Ave. No.
New Hope, MN 55428
(612) 533-2449

Open to job seekers, spouses and partners. Meets Tuesdays, 8—9:30 a.m. Group focuses on networking and group sharing. Guest speakers invited on alternate weeks. Drop in. No charge.

DAKOTA COUNTY EMPLOYMENT & TRAINING
Training Center West
14551 County Road 11
Burnsville, MN 55337
(612) 953-3400

Job support group for agency clients. Assists participants with primary job-seeking skills, networking, cold calling, interviewing, on-going job-seeking support. Call for eligibility requirements. No charge.

EAST SIDE NEIGHBORHOOD SERVICE, INC.
Job Search Workshop
1929 Second St. N.E.
Minneapolis, MN 55418
(612) 781-6011

Open to the public. Series of job-search workshops with speakers and small group discussion. Call for information. No charge.

FIRST EVANGELICAL LUTHERAN CHURCH
Jobs in Transition 'n Support Group
4000 Linden Street
White Bear Lake, MN 55110
(612) 429-9594

Open to the public. Meets Mondays, 7—9 p.m. Weekly meetings with informational speakers, small-group discussions, networking opportunities. Database of participants and employers. Access to typewriters and computers. Drop in. No charge.

40 PLUS OF MINNESOTA
Job Support Group

(612) 683-9898

Open to the public but targeted to experienced management, technical, and executive-level individuals. Meets Tuesdays, 7—9 p.m. Call for location. Weekly meetings with opportunity to enter focused career development and support programs offering skills assessments, marketing teamwork. Forty Plus is networked through a federation of 22 Minnesota professional associations, and 40 Plus groups nationwide. Call for information. No charge.

GRACE LUTHERAN CHURCH
Jobs in Transition 'n Support Group

13655 Round Lake Blvd.
Andover, MN 55304
(612) 421-6520

Open to the public. Meets Thursdays, 7—9 p.m. Provides access to computers for word processing and maintains a database of job seekers for a job matching program. Guest speakers are invited on alternate weeks. Drop in. No charge.

HIRED
Job Club

Robbinsdale Community Center
4139 Regent Ave. No.
Robbinsdale, MN 55422
(612) 536-0777

Open only to participants of HIRED's employment programs by counselor referral. Meets Tuesdays at 9 a.m. Provides information, motivation, support. Guest speakers on job application process, interviewing, and other job seeking skills. No charge.

JOB SUPPORT GROUPS

HOLY NAME OF JESUS CHURCH
Holy Name Network

155 County Rd. 24
Wayzata, MN 55391
(612) 473-7901

Call for schedule. For job seekers and employed professionals who wish to give and receive peer support, information, and networking leads. Some formal job search programming. Drop in. No charge.

PAX CHRISTI CATHOLIC COMMUNITY
In Transition

12100 Pioneer Trail
Eden Prairie, MN 55347
(612) 941-3150

Open to job seekers, spouses and partners. Meets first and third Sundays, 7—8:30 p.m. Group offers general discussion, support, job-search direction, information sharing, networking opportunities. Guest speakers once a month. Drop in. No charge.

PILLSBURY NEIGHBORHOOD SERVICES, INC.
Job Seeker's Support Group

Coyle Center
420 15th Ave. So.
Minneapolis, MN 55454
(612) 338-5282

Open to Minneapolis residents. Informal discussions about unemployment and job-search issues. Call for information. No charge.

ST. ALPHONSUS CHURCH JOB CLUB

CCD Building
4111 71st Ave. No.
Brooklyn Center, MN 55429
(612) 561-5100

Open to the public. Meets Mondays, 9 a.m. Group provides mutual support, information, strategies, and job leads. Drop in. No charge.

ST. ANDREW LUTHERAN CHURCH
Job Transition Group

14100 Valley View Road
Eden Prairie, MN 55344
(612) 937-2776

Open to the public. Meets Wednesdays, 11:30 a.m. Participants provide support and networking tips, and share updates about their personal job search. Call for new address, spring, 1994. No charge.

ST. EDWARDS CATHOLIC CHURCH
Job Transition Group

9401 Nesbitt Ave. So.
Bloomington, MN 55437
(612) 835-7101

Open to the public. Meets second and fourth Tuesdays, 7:30—9 p.m. Informal meetings provide support and networking. Occasional speakers. Drop in or call for information. No charge.

ST. GERARD'S CHURCH
Job in Transition 'n Support Group

9600 Regent Ave. No.
Brooklyn Park, MN 55443
(612) 424-8770

Open to the public. Led by professional career consultant. Meets Tuesdays, 7—9 p.m. Focuses on active job-search strategies and support. Also sponsors confidential resume referral service. No charge.

ST. JAMES LUTHERAN CHURCH
Career Continuation Support Group

3650 Williams Drive
Burnsville, MN 55337
(612) 890-4534

Meets Sundays, September—May, at 8:15 a.m. Presentations on job-search techniques, grief due to job loss, resume preparation, interviewing, emotional and spiritual support. Drop in. No charge.

JOB SUPPORT GROUPS

ST. JOAN OF ARC CATHOLIC CHURCH
Job Support Group

4500 Clinton Ave. So.
Minneapolis, MN 55409
(612) 823-8205

Open to the public. Meets Mondays, 6:30—8:30 p.m. Small-group discussions with a spiritual focus for emotional support. Alternate weekly meetings feature guest speakers. No charge.

ST. JOHN NEUMANN CATHOLIC CHURCH
Job Transition Support Group

4030 Pilot Knob Road
Eagan, MN 55122
(612) 454-2079

Open to the public. Meets first and third Thursdays of the month, 7—9 p.m. Offers guest speakers, group discussion, human resources panel, computer and word processing skills development, resume improvement. Drop in. No charge.

ST. STEVEN'S EPISCOPAL CHURCH
Job Transition Group

4439 West 50th Street
Edina, MN 55424
(612) 920-0595

Open to the public. Meets six times per year. Meetings include speakers, discussion, one-on-one mentorship, networking opportunities, spiritual and personal support, practical job search guidance. Call for schedule. No charge.

This chapter continues on the following page.

TAPS' JOB CLUB
Training Applicants for Placement Success

777 Raymond Ave.
St. Paul, MN 55114
(612) 646-8675   (800) 779-0777

Targeted to people with epilepsy. Meets Tuesdays, 10—11:30 a.m. Guest speakers, group discussion, peer counseling covering a wide range of employment issues. Call for information and to schedule an appointment prior to attending. Sponsored by Epilepsy Foundations of Minnesota and America. No charge.

TEMPLE ISRAEL
Job Support Program

2324 Emerson Ave. So.
Minneapolis, MN 55405
(612) 377-8680

Meets Wednesdays, 7 p.m. Workshop orientation focused on resume-writing, interviewing and networking. Drop in. No charge.

TWIN CITIES MEN'S CENTER (TMC)

3255 Hennepin Ave. So., Suite 55
Minneapolis, MN 55408
(612) 822-5892

Workshops and on-going support groups focusing on transition issues. All groups open to men; some targeted to men and women. Call for information and St. Paul location. Free or voluntary donation.

TWIN CITY PURCHASING MANAGEMENT ASSOCIATION
Employment Transition Group

(612) 379-0733

For members only. Generally meets prior to Association meetings, third Thursday of the month, September—May. Provides support, networking opportunities, and speakers on job-search strategies. Locations change monthly. Call for current location.

WAYZATA COMMUNITY CHURCH
Career Transition Support Group

Ferndale & Wayzata Blvd.
Wayzata, MN 55391
(612) 473-8876

Open to the public. Structured seven-week course combines formal presentations on job-search skills, strategies, emotional stress, and financial issues with small group discussions. Offered twice per year. Call for information. No charge.

WOODDALE CHURCH
Job Transition Ministry

6630 Shady Oak Road
Eden Prairie, MN 55344
(612) 944-6300

Open to the public. Meets Mondays, 7:15—8:15 a.m. The group offers the opportunity to exchange networking contacts and job leads, and share resources. A skills seminar is offered once every other month. Drop in. No charge.

WOMENVENTURE
Job Search Support Group for Women

2324 University Ave. W., Suite 200
St. Paul, MN 55114
(612) 646-3808

Open to the public. Meets Tuesdays, 10—11:30 a.m., and Wednesday evenings, 6—7:30 p.m. Facilitated group for women offers on-going encouragement during the job search. Drop in. No charge.

Networking Organizations

Call it Who You Know. Call it Clout. Call it Contacts. Your network of old friends, new friends, acquaintances, co-workers, and relatives can help you get hired.

Networking is the art of expanding your contacts to eventually reach a potential employer. Case in point: Seventy percent of all job seekers directly contact employers to inquire about unadvertised positions. How do they know about these jobs?

Networking. And it works.

Make a list of everyone you know. Neighbors. Former classmates. Past employers. Church members. Sorority sisters. Then, don't be shy about passing the word along that you're looking for work. Ask these contacts for introductions to anyone they know who may have a lead to a job opening in your field. Follow up on all referrals.

Business, civic, and professional organizations are also useful for expanding your network. Become a visible participant at the associations that serve your profession or industry, and at community, church, volunteer, and civic organizations.

The listings that follow represent only a sampling of state and local associations. Those included provide some type of job seeking assistance to members. To track down other networking organizations, check your local library for the Directory of Minnesota Business and Professional Associations ($35), published by James J. Hill Reference Library, 80 W. Fourth St., St. Paul, MN 55102, (612) 227-9531. This 90-page directory identifies about 350 Minnesota trade associations and professional societies.

NETWORKING ORGANIZATIONS

See also Chapter Four for national associations providing job-search assistance.

AIA MINNESOTA
275 Market St., Suite 54
Minneapolis, MN 55405
(612) 338-6763

Professional association for architects. Offers job bank of current job openings and resume referral service. Membership not required.

APICS—TWIN CITIES
Educational Society for Resource Management
10313 Virginia Road
Bloomington, MN 55438
(612) 941-7305   Fax—(612) 941-8668

Serving individuals in materials/operations management in purchasing, manufacturing, shipping, receiving, production/inventory control, data processing, and information systems. Offers resume file service. Job vacancies are announced at meetings. Annual dues, $85.

AMERICAN MARKETING ASSOCIATION
MINNESOTA CHAPTER
4248 Park Glen Road
Minneapolis, MN 55416
(612) 927-4262

Serving professionals in marketing, market research, and sales. Provides educational and networking services. Distributes listings of job openings to members. National organization also publishes job vacancies.

AMERICAN SOCIETY OF MECHANICAL ENGINEERS
555 Park Street
St. Paul, MN 55103
(612) 942-1340—Minnesota Chapter   (800) 628-6437—Membership

Serving mechanical engineers. Offers regional/national job bulletin, computer job bank, publications, reduced meeting fees and dues abatement for unemployed members, job fairs, free resume referral service, on-line service to investigate career opportunities.

AMERICAN SOCIETY OF WOMEN ACCOUNTANTS
TWIN CITIES CHAPTER
10488 Washington Blvd. N.E.
Blaine, MN 55434
(612) 755-1608

Professional association for women accountants. Membership publications include job listings and positions wanted ads.

CHAMBERS OF COMMERCE

Many chambers of commerce publish lists identifying local networking organizations. Below is a sampling of Minnesota and Wisconsin chambers. Refer to your area phone directory for other chamber offices.

BEMIDJI CHAMBER
300 Bemidji, P.O. Box 850
Bemidji, MN 56601
(218) 751-3541   (800) 458-2223

Organizations list, $6.

DULUTH CHAMBER
118 E. Superior Street
Duluth, MN 55802
(218) 722-5501

Free list of organizations.

EAU CLAIRE, WI CHAMBER
505 S. Dewey, Suite 101
Eau Claire, MN 54701
(715) 834-1204   (800) 944-2449

Organizations list, $11.

FARIBAULT CHAMBER
530 Wilson Ave., P.O. Box 434
Faribault, MN 55021
(507) 334-4381   (800) 658-2354

Organizations list, $25.

GRAND RAPIDS CHAMBER
One N.W. Third Street
Grand Rapids, MN 55144
(218) 326-6619   (800) 472-6366

Free list of organizations.

HIBBING CHAMBER
211 E. Howard Street
Hibbing, MN 55746
(218) 262-3897   (800) 4-442-2464

Free list of organizations.

LA CROSSE, WI CHAMBER
712 Main Street
La Crosse, WI 54601
(608) 784-4880

Organizations list, $1.50.

MANKATO CHAMBER
220 E. Main
Mankato, MN 56001
(507) 345-4519

Free list of organizations.

NETWORKING ORGANIZATIONS

CHAMBERS OF COMMERCE cont.

MENOMONIE, WI CHAMBER
533 N. Broadway, P.O. Box 246
Menomonie, WI 54751
(715) 235-9087   (800) 283-1862

Free list of organizations.

MOORHEAD CHAMBER
725 Center Avenue
Moorhead, MN 56560
(218) 236-6200

Organizations list, $4.

OWATONNA CHAMBER
320 Hoffman Drive
Owatonna, MN 55060
(507) 451-7970   (800) 423-6466

Organizations list, $10.

ROCHESTER CHAMBER
220 S. Broadway, Suite 100
Rochester, MN 55904
(507) 288-1122

Organizations list, $10.

ST. CLOUD CHAMBER
30 Sixth Ave. South
St. Cloud, MN 56302
(612) 251-2940

Organizations list, $2.

SUPERIOR, WI CHAMBER
305 E. Second Street
Superior, WI 54880
(715) 394-7716   (800) 942-5313

Free list of organizations.

HRP OF MINNESOTA
1711 W. County Road B, Suite 300-N
Roseville, MN 55113
(612) 635-0306   Fax—(612) 635-0307

Serving human resource professionals. Offers networking opportunities, continuing education, positions available/wanted ads in member publications. Annual dues, $35.

MEETING PLANNERS INTERNATIONAL
MINNESOTA CHAPTER
(612) 470-7838

Serving meeting planners, hospitality industry, caterers and suppliers. National association provides access to career counselors at annual conference, industry salary surveys. Annual dues, $260.

This chapter continues on the following page.

MIDWEST DIRECT MARKETING ASSOCIATION
4248 Park Glen Road
Minneapolis, MN 55416
(612) 927-9220   Fax—(612) 929-1318

Serving direct marketing professionals. Offers resume referral service, networking opportunities. Job vacancies published in member publications. Annual dues, $75.

MINNESOTA BROADCASTERS ASSOCIATION
3517 Raleigh Ave. So.
P.O. Box 16030
St. Louis Park, MN 55416
(612) 926-8123

Serving members of broadcasting industry. Offers resume referral service, and positions wanted ads in monthly newsletter. Membership not required for these services.

MINNESOTA BUSINESS BREAKFASTS
Edinborough Park
7700 York Avenue So.
Edina, MN 55435
Reservations: (612) 553-1122   Fax—(612) 553-9092

Networking opportunity open to the public. Meets monthly on second and fourth Tuesdays, 7:15—9 a.m. at Edinborough Park. Programs focus on sales and marketing skills with ideas to help non-sales personnel sharpen job-search skills. Networking encouraged. Call for details. Tickets, $15 at door, $12 in advance.

MINNESOTA RECREATION & PARK ASSOCIATION
5005 West 36th Street
St. Louis Park, MN 55416
(612) 920-6906

Serving recreation, park and community education professionals. Publishes monthly jobs bulletin identifying 25—100 openings nationwide. Free to members; non-member subscription, $25/year.

NETWORKING ORGANIZATIONS

MINNESOTA SOCIETY OF CERTIFIED PUBLIC ACCOUNTANTS
7900 Xerxes Ave. So., Suite 1230
Bloomington, MN 55431
(612) 831-2707

Serving certified public accountants. Offers job matching service to members only.

MINNESOTA SOCIETY OF PROFESSIONAL ENGINEERS
555 Park St., Suite 130
St. Paul, MN 55103
(612) 292-8860

Serving registered engineers in all disciplines. Monthly membership magazine includes 10—12 job listings per issue.

MINNESOTA TELECOMMUNICATIONS ASSOCIATION
9851 Crestwood Terrace
Minneapolis, MN 55347
(612) 934-8499—General
(612) 671-7333—Job Hotline

Serving telecommunications industry. Offers networking opportunities, job hotline, continuing education. Open to members and non-members. Annual dues, $100.

MINNESOTA WOMEN IN THE TRADES
550 Rice Street
St. Paul, MN 55103
(612) 228-9955—General
(612) 228-1271—Job Hotline

Serving women in non-traditional employment such as firefighters, mechanics, drafters, machinists, service technicians, individuals in construction, building trades, etc. Offers job hotline, resume referral service, job matching program, networking opportunities. Call for schedule. Annual dues, $25.

NATIONAL ASSOCIATION OF SOCIAL WORKERS
480 Concordia Avenue
St. Paul, MN 55103
(612) 293-1935

Professional association serving members only. Monthly job opportunities bulletin with 10—30 job openings for professional social workers. Accepts paid advertising for positions wanted. Submit self-addressed stamped envelope.

NATIONAL SOCIETY FOR PERFORMANCE AND INSTRUCTION
MINNESOTA CHAPTER
4709 Victoria Street
Shoreview, MN 55126

Serving professionals in training and development, instruction design, performance technology. Offers job bank, resume referral service. Job vacancies announced at meetings. Publishes directory of independent consultants. Write for information. Annual dues, $35.

PRINTING INDUSTRY OF MINNESOTA INC.
450 North Syndicate, Suite 200
St. Paul, MN 55104
(612) 646-4826

Trade association serving Minnesota printing and graphic arts industry. Provides career materials and resume referral service to job seekers at all levels. Membership not required for these services.

PROFESSIONAL ASSOCIATION FOR OCCUPATIONAL THERAPISTS IN MINNESOTA
P.O. Box 26532
Minneapolis, MN 55426
(612) 920-0484   Fax—(612) 920-6098

Serving practitioners of occupational therapy. Placement service includes bi-weekly announcements of job vacancies at nominal charge to members only. Call for information.

NETWORKING ORGANIZATIONS

PUBLIC RELATIONS SOCIETY OF AMERICA
MINNESOTA CHAPTER
P.O. Box 580321
Minneapolis, MN 55458
(612) 338-7772

Serving public relations practitioners. Offers resume referral service to members, free for limited time. Non-members, $25.

SALES AND MARKETING EXECUTIVES
2626 E. 82nd St., Suite 201
Minneapolis, MN 55425
(612) 854-0109   Fax—(612) 854-1402

Serving executive level sales and marketing management. Provides networking meetings, job bank, positions available/wanted ads in member publications. Call for information.

SOCIETY FOR MARKETING PROFESSIONAL SERVICES
9464 New Castle Road
Woodbury, MN 55125
(612) 739-2161

Twin Cities chapter of national association serving professionals in building/construction industry: architects, engineers, general contractors, construction management, interior design. Job bank, free to members. Non-member fee, $25/3 months.

SOCIETY FOR TECHNICAL COMMUNICATIONS
TWIN CITIES CHAPTER
(612) 338-1058

Serving technical communicators. Offers job bank, employment referral service, networking opportunities. Job vacancies announced at meetings. Annual dues, $85.

This chapter continues on the following page.

TWIN CITIES PERSONNEL ASSOCIATION
7630 W. 145 St., Suite 202
Apple Valley, MN 55124
(612) 432-7755—General
(612) 832-3898—Job Hotline

Serving human resource professionals. Networking meetings open to members and non-members. Offers continuing education, job hotline. Annual dues, $50.

TWIN CITIES QUALITY ASSURANCE ASSOCIATION
P.O. Box 2799 Loop Station
Minneapolis, MN 55402
(612) 440-6300   Fax—(612) 440-5700

Serving software quality assurance professionals. Provides resume referral service, networking opportunities. Job vacancies announced at monthly meetings. Annual dues, $25.

TWIN CITY PURCHASING MANAGEMENT ASSOCIATION
2021 East Hennepin Ave., Suite 375
Minneapolis, MN 55413
(612) 379-0733

Serving purchasing and material management personnel. Offers resume referral service (membership not required), and monthly employment transition group for members only. Call for schedule.

WOMEN IN COMMUNICATIONS, INC.
13636 Marigold St. N.W.
Minneapolis, MN 55304
(612) 323-3393

Serving professional women in communications. Offers resume referral service, free to members; $25, non-members. Resume critique service, $10. Monthly networking meetings, annual career seminar for college students and career changers. Write or call for information.

CRISIS & REFERRAL HELPLINES

TELEPHONE HELPLINES
&
CRISIS REFERRALS

Losing a job puts many folks on an emotional roller coaster. It's not uncommon to feel shocked. Angry. Isolated. Hurt. Depressed. Sad. Or a gamut of other emotions. Sometimes the stress contributes to marital tensions or chemical dependency. Perhaps you require immediate assistance with food, housing, child care or other basic needs. Luckily, there is no shortage of helplines in Minnesota or Wisconsin.

If you feel the need for professional counseling, the best place to start may be with your own health care provider, especially if you are a member of an HMO. Some plans require that mental health services be received at specific contracted clinics. If you comply with their requirements, services may be free or at a nominal cost. If you do not have insurance, you still may have options that are free or available on a sliding fee scale.

For those in crisis now: Many hotlines and helplines will refer you to community-based support services for immediate assistance. Others provide 24-hour crisis counseling. See also Resources for Basic Needs, beginning on page 206.

NATIONWIDE

ALCOHOLICS ANONYMOUS
(800) 252-6465

Telephone referrals to AA meeting locations nationwide, 24 hours.

HAZELDEN INFORMATION CENTER
Box 11
Center City, MN 55012
(800) 257-7800

Telephone helpline. Referrals to local and national treatment programs or self-help meetings for chemical dependency and other addictions. Phones answered daily, 7 a.m. to 11:30 p.m.

TWIN CITIES

ALCOHOLICS ANONYMOUS INTERGROUP

WEST METRO
Calls answered 24 hours.
6300 Walker St., Suite 212
St. Louis Park, MN 55416
(612) 922-0880

EAST METRO
Open weekdays and Sundays
951 E. 5th Street
St. Paul, MN 55106
(612) 227-5502

Telephone helpline and referrals. For anyone with a desire to stop drinking. Referrals to local meeting locations.

CHILD CARE RESOURCE AND REFERRAL LINES
- (612) 783-4884—Anoka County
- (612) 496-2321—Carver/Scott Counties
- (612) 431-7752—Dakota County
- (612) 341-2066—Hennepin County
- (612) 641-0332—Ramsey County
- (612) 430-6488—Washington County

Referral helpline. Conducts customized searches for child care based on client's criteria. Call for information. Fees may apply.

CRISIS & REFERRAL HELPLINES

CHRYSALIS
2650 Nicollet Ave. So.
Minneapolis, MN 55408
(612) 871-2603

Volunteer-staffed telephone helpline and walk-in counseling service. Targeted to women, age 18 and up. Referrals to support groups, legal assistance. Free or low-cost.

CRISIS CONNECTION
P.O. Box 14958
Minneapolis, MN 55414
(612) 379-6363   Fax—(612) 379-6391

Telephone helpline. Open 24 hours. Crisis intervention and counseling, suicide prevention, information and referrals to community resources. Nighttime outreach (team of two counselors meet at client's home or public location for crisis intervention).

FIRST CALL FOR HELP

WEST METRO
Open 24 hours
404 So. 8th Street
Minneapolis, MN 55404
(612) 335-5000

EAST METRO
Open 8 a.m.—8 p.m.
166 E. 4th St., Suite 310
St. Paul, MN 55101
(612) 224-1133

Telephone helpline. Comprehensive referral service with extensive listings for crisis counseling centers, social services, health care. Upon request, makes effort to link callers to free or low-cost services.

GAY AND LESBIAN HELPLINE
310 E. 38th St., Suite 204
Minneapolis, MN 55409
(612) 822-8661   (800) 800-0907

Crisis and referral helpline. Open M—F, noon to midnight; Saturdays, 4 p.m. to midnight. Information and referrals, crisis and support counseling. Serving Minnesota and western Wisconsin.

HSI CRISIS CLINICS
Human Services Inc.
7066 Stillwater Blvd. No.
Oakdale, MN 55128
(612) 777-5222

Twenty-four hour crisis helpline and walk-in counseling. Staff includes psychiatrists, nurses, psychologists, social workers and mental health workers. Referrals provided as needed.

LOVE LINES, INC.
2701 S.E. 4th Street
Minneapolis, MN 55414
(612) 379-1199

Telephone helpline. Free 24-hour crisis service. Also offers in-person counseling on appointment basis. Sponsored by Christian ministry.

PERSPECTIVES, INC.
17717 Highway 7
Minnetonka, MN 55345
(612) 474-5443

Telephone information and referral. Walk-in mental health service provided by trained peer counselors. Offers personal growth and self-esteem classes, workshops, support groups.

SENIOR LINKAGE LINE
2021 E. Hennepin Ave., #130
Minneapolis, MN 55413
(612) 224-0044—East Metro
(612) 824-9999—West Metro
(800) 333-2433

Referral helpline for seniors, ages 50 and up. Open business hours. Referrals to community and job-seeking services.

CRISIS & REFERRAL HELPLINES

NORTHERN MINNESOTA

ARROWHEAD ECONOMIC OPPORTUNITY AGENCY
702 Third Ave. So.
Virginia, MN 55792
(800) 662-5711

Referral helpline and social service agency. Serving Koochiching, St. Louis, Lake, Cook, Itasca, Carlton and Aitkin Counties.

BI-COUNTY COMMUNITY ACTION
P.O. Box 579
Bemidji, MN 56601
(800) 332-7161

Referral helpline. Serving Beltrami and Cass Counties. Assistance with fuel, rent, and family services.

FIRST CALL FOR HELP
P.O. Box 113
Grand Rapids, MN 55744
(218) 326-8565   (800) 442-8565—Regional only

Crisis and referral helpline, answered 24 hours. Serving Itasca and Koochiching Counties. Crisis intervention, active listening and referral.

HUMAN DEVELOPMENT CENTER
1401 E. First Street
Duluth, MN 55812
(800) 634-8775

Crisis and referral helpline serving northeastern Minnesota. Provides 24-hour mental health counseling.

INTER COUNTY COMMUNITY COUNCIL
P.O. Box 189
Oklee, MN 56742
(218) 796-5144

Referral helpline. Calls answered M—F. Serving Red Lake, Pennington, East Polk, Clear Water Counties. Assistance with food, energy, repairs.

MINNESOTA JOB SEEKER'S SOURCEBOOK

MILLER DWAN MEDICAL CENTER CRISIS LINE
502 E. Second Street
Duluth, MN 55802
(218) 723-0099   (800) 766-8762

Crisis and referral 24-hour helpline. Serving St. Louis County. Phone assistance, direct referrals to crisis team. No charge for call, but $150 initial cost for crisis team counseling.

ST. LOUIS COUNTY SOCIAL SERVICES
Information and Referral
Government Service Center, Room 109
320 W. Second Street
Duluth, MN 55802
(218) 726-2222   (800) 232-1300

Referral helpline. Open business hours. Serving St. Louis and Lake Counties. Referrals to social services.

TRI-VALLEY OPPORTUNITY COUNCIL
102 No. Broadway
P.O. Box 607
Crookston, MN 56716
(800) 584-7020

Referral helpline. Answered business hours, M—F. Serving Norman, Polk, Marshall Counties. Referrals to social services including financial counseling, child care, fuel assistance.

CENTRAL MINNESOTA

FIRST CALL FOR HELP
26 No. Sixth Avenue
St. Cloud, MN 56302
(612) 252-3474   (800) 828-5709

Telephone helpline and referral service, answered M—F, 24 hours. Serving Morrison, Stearns, Benton, Sherburne, Wright, Mille Lacs, and Todd Counties. Listings for crisis counseling, support.

CRISIS & REFERRAL HELPLINES

ALCOHOLICS ANONYMOUS ASSISTANCE LINE
St. Cloud, MN
(612) 253-8183

Telephone helpline. For anyone with a desire to stop drinking. Calls answered 24 hours.

CARITAS FAMILY SERVICES
Catholic Charities
305 No. 7th Ave.
St. Cloud, MN 56303
(612) 252-4121

Crisis intervention and assistance. Provides counseling and short-term assistance. Food shelf, clothing, and household items available to individuals or families in financial crisis. Call for appointment. Free.

FAMILY RESOURCE CENTER HELPLINE
30620 Olinda Trail No.
Lindstrom, MN 55045
(612) 257-2400   (800) 747-2400

Referral helpline. Open business hours. Serving Chisago, Isanti, Kanabec, Mille Lacs, and Pine Counties. Referrals to social services, food shelves, housing, legal, and debt assistance.

HEARTLAND COMMUNITY ACTION AGENCY
310 So. First Street
P.O. Box 1359
Willmar, MN 56201
(612) 235-0850   (800) 992-1710

Referral helpline and social service agency. Open business hours. Serving Meeker, Renville, Kandiyohi and McLeod Counties. Referrals to social services.

This chapter continues on the following page.

LAKE COUNTRY INFORMATION LINE
P.O. Box 54
Fergus Falls, MN 56538
(218) 736-2856   (800) 257-5463   TDD—(218) 736-3372

Referral helpline. Open business hours. Serving Becker, Douglas, Grant, Otter Tail, Wadena, and Wilkin Counties. Referrals to community social services.

LUTHERAN SOCIAL SERVICES
343 Third Ave. So.
St. Cloud, MN 56301
(612) 251-7700

Referral helpline directs callers to agency services including individual and group counseling for families, couples and individuals.

PRAIRIE 5 COMMUNITY ACTION COUNCIL, INC.
7th Street and Washington Avenue
P.O. Box 695
Montevideo, MN 56265-0695
(612) 269-7976   (800) 292-5437

Referral helpline. Open business hours. Serving Yellow Medicine, Big Stone, Chippewa, Lac qui Parle, and Swift Counties. Referrals to social services for fuel assistance, family self-sufficiency programs.

THE CRISIS LINE
1321 No. 13th Street
St. Cloud, MN 56303
(612) 253-5555   (800) 635-8008

Crisis helpline. Calls answered 24 hours. Serving Benton, Sherburne, Stearns, Wright Counties. Handles alcohol, drug or mental health emergencies through the Central Minnesota Mental Health Center.

CRISIS & REFERRAL HELPLINES

WEST CENTRAL MINNESOTA COMMUNITIES ACTION
17 E. Division
P.O. Box 127
Elbow Lake, MN 56531
(218) 685-4486   (800) 492-4805

Referral helpline. Open business hours. Serving Pope, Stevens, Traverse, Grant, Douglas Counties. Referrals to community social services.

SOUTHERN MINNESOTA

BLUE EARTH INFORMATION AND REFERRAL
Mankato, MN
(507) 389-8374

Referral helpline. Open business hours. Serving greater Mankato, including Blue Earth and Brown Counties.

CONTACT
(507) 451-9100   (800) 648-2330

Crisis and referral helpline. Serving greater Owatonna, Steele, and Waseca Counties. Counseling and referrals to social services.

FIRST CALL FOR HELP
Northfield Community Action Center
1001 Division
Northfield, MN 55057
(507) 645-9301   (800) 200-INFO (local only)

Referral helpline. Open business hours. Serving Rice County. Referrals to social services, emergency, food, and housing assistance.

MINNESOTA VALLEY ACTION COUNCIL
(800) 767-7139

Referral helpline. Open business hours. Serving Waseca, Faribault, Le Sueur, Martin, Nicollet, Sibley, and Watonwan Counties. Referrals to fuel assistance, employment, food, transportation, housing, loans.

SE MINNESOTA INFORMATION AND REFERRAL
326 So. Broadway, Suite D
Albert Lea, MN 56007
(800) 277-8418

Referral helpline. Open business hours. Serving Dodge, Freeborn, Goodhue, Mower, Olmstead, Steele, Wabasha, Houston, and Rice Counties. Referrals to community day care and other services.

SOUTHWEST OPPORTUNITY COUNCIL
515 Tenth Street
Worthington, MN 56187
(800) 658-2444

Referral helpline. Answered business hours. Serving Murray, Nobles, Pipestone, and Rock Counties. Referrals to social services, emergency housing, child care, energy assistance.

WESTERN COMMUNITY ACTION
203 W. Main
Marshall, MN 56258
(507) 537-1416   (800) 658-2448

Referral helpline. Open business hours. Serving Cottonwood, Jackson, Lincoln, Lyon, and Redwood Counties. Referrals to social services, transportation, fuel assistance.

WESTERN WISCONSIN

AREA INFORMATION AND REFERRAL SERVICE
L.E. Phillips Memorial Public Library
400 Eau Claire Street
Eau Claire, WI 54701
(715) 839-5004   TDD (715) 839-1689

Information and referral to area community services. Answered daily, Monday through Saturday. Serving Eau Claire County.

CRISIS & REFERRAL HELPLINES

FIRST CALL FOR HELP
La Crosse, WI
(800) 362-8255

Crisis and referral helpline, answered 24 hours. Serving Wisconsin counties of La Crosse, Buffalo, Trempealeau, Jackson, Monroe, and Vernon; Minnesota counties of Fillmore, Houston, and Winona. Referrals to day care, free health clinics, legal, and financial services.

WEST CENTRAL WISCONSIN COMMUNITY ACTION AGENCY
525 Second Street
Glenwood City, WI 54013
(715) 265-4271

Referral helpline. Open business hours. Serving Barron, Chippewa, Dunn, Pepin, Polk, St. Croix, and Pierce Counties. Referrals to social services such as small business development program, low-income weatherization, housing and other social services.

Resources
For
Basic Needs

Health Care Coverage
Housing
Food
Legal Concerns
Credit, Debt & Budgeting Problems

If you are experiencing problems with money management, health care coverage, legal problems including foreclosure, or other concerns about meeting basic needs because you're unemployed, there are many organizations that can provide counseling and assistance.

Most referral helplines listed in the preceding section will refer you to local community services that provide assistance. However, on the following pages we've identified some direct sources you can tap on your own to get the help you need. Most services listed in this section are free or low-cost to eligible clients.

Because we know that health care can be a challenge for those in job transition we've tracked down programs which may offer solutions. If you're facing a financial crisis, the budget counseling services that follow can help improve your money management techniques, or intervene on your behalf to negotiate a payment plan with creditors.

Legal problems may also arise due to a job loss, in areas related to credit, child support abatement, unemployment, wrongful discharge, bankruptcy, foreclosure, or eviction. And basic needs like food and housing cannot be overlooked. There's help available.

RESOURCES FOR BASIC NEEDS

HEALTH CARE

COBRA

COBRA, which stands for Consolidated Omnibus Budget Reconciliation Act, is a federal law which allows you, under specific circumstances, to continue to buy group health insurance through your former employer for 18 months up to three years

You may be eligible for COBRA if you are:

- Unemployed or if the number of hours you work has been reduced.
- An employee who accepted a new job with a new health plan that limits coverage of pre-existing conditions including pregnancy.
- A dependent of a deceased worker.
- A divorced spouse of an employee.
- Losing your status as a "dependent child" under the employer's health plan rules.

Under this federal law, you are included if you worked for an employer with more than 20 employees on at least 50 percent of the working days in the previous calendar year and who offered health plans. The law does not apply to the federal government and certain church-related organizations. Coverage provided under COBRA must be identical to that provided to current employees, but the employer can charge up to 102 percent of the group premium.

MINNESOTACARE

444 Lafayette Road No.
St. Paul, MN 55155
(612) 297-3862   (800) 657-3672

MinnesotaCare is a comprehensive family healthcare plan designed for permanent Minnesota residents who are uninsured, ineligible for other medical assistance, and who meet specific income guidelines. Premiums are based on income and family size. Call for eligibility guidelines and application.

This chapter continues on the following page.

HILL-BURTON FACILITIES

(800) 638-0742

In 1946, Congress passed a law which gave hospitals money for construction and modernization. In return, the facilities that received these Hill-Burton funds agreed to provide a reasonable volume of free services to persons unable to pay. Hill-Burton facilities must provide a specific amount of free care to qualified individuals each year, but may stop once they have reached that amount. Eligibility for free services is based on income guidelines.

Many Minnesota and Wisconsin hospitals are Hill-Burton facilities. To obtain a list of facilities in your community, call the hotline above.

COMMUNITY CLINIC CONSORTIUM

450 No. Syndicate, Suite 70
St. Paul, MN 55104
(612) 644-6555

Referral helpline. Targeted to medically uninsured, underinsured, and underserved individuals. Referrals are made to community health centers in the Twin Cities seven-county metro area that provide medical, dental and mental health services. Eligibility is based on income guidelines and family size. Call for information. Sliding fee.

HEALTH HELPLINES

Children's On Call

CHILDREN'S HOSPITAL OF ST. PAUL

(612) 220-6868

A registered nurse answers questions on child/adolescent behavior and medical problems.

445-CARE

ST. FRANCIS REGIONAL MEDICAL CENTER

(612) 445-2273

Provides physician referrals and the opportunity to talk with a registered nurse for health information. Answered 24 hours.

RESOURCES FOR BASIC NEEDS

HealthSpan MedFormation

(612) 863-3333

Provides physician referrals and information on health screenings, classes and programs, as well as taped messages on a variety of health concerns. Also offers opportunity to talk with registered nurse.

Tel-Med

ST. PAUL RAMSEY MEDICAL CENTER

(612) 221-8686

Recorded information on health-related topics in 29 major categories.

Tele-Health

HEALTHEAST

(612) 232-2600

Provides physician referrals and opportunity to talk with registered nurse for information. No medical advice given.

University Health Line

UNIVERSITY OF MINNESOTA HOSPITAL AND CLINIC

(612) 626-6000

Helpline provides recorded health information and opportunity to speak to a registered nurse. Physician referrals provided. Free.

UNIVERSITY OF MINNESOTA DENTAL CLINIC

515 Delaware St. S.E.
Minneapolis, MN 55455
(612) 625-2495

Dental clinic. Open to the public with some eligibility guidelines. Offers savings up to 25—35 percent on wide range of dental services. Call for information.

This chapter continues on the following page.

HOUSING

AFFORDABLE HOUSING HOTLINE
The Connection

(612) 922-9000

Twenty-four hour telephone helpline provides callers with listings for Twin Cities rental properties based on caller's needs. Also provides information about Section 8 and subsidized housing. Properties are not pre-screened. Information is provided by property owners. Free.

FOOD

FARE SHARE
Ramsey Action Programs

807 Hampden Avenue
St. Paul, MN 55114
(612) 644-9339
(800) 582-4291

Fare Share is part of a worldwide network allowing individuals to exchange two hours of volunteer service, plus $14, for grocery packages containing meat, produce, condiments and dry goods at a 60% savings. Food is distributed monthly at host sites in Minnesota and Wisconsin. Registration and payment in advance is required. Call for information about site locations.

MINNESOTA FOOD SHELF ASSOCIATION

4025 W. Broadway Avenue
Robbinsdale, MN 55422
(612) 536-9180
(800) 782-6372

Referral helpline. Information and referrals to approximately 330 Minnesota food shelves. Call for information.

RESOURCES FOR BASIC NEEDS

LEGAL ASSISTANCE

TEL LAW
Hennepin County Bar Association
(612) 332-2114

Information and referral line. Extensive recorded information, accessible 24 hours, provides referrals to free and other legal services statewide. Also offers informative messages on topics such as employment law, bankruptcy, home ownership, civil law, family law, criminal law, landlord/tenant rights, wills and estate planning, consumer concerns, juvenile law, and tax law. Free.

MINNESOTA DEPARTMENT OF HUMAN RIGHTS
500 Bremer Tower
7th Place & Minnesota Street
St. Paul, MN 55101
(612) 296-5663

Legal assistance for individuals with employment discrimination claims. Services include investigation of claims, filing charges, seeking remedies. Representatives hold office hours in many Minnesota communities. Call or write for information.

FINANCIAL COUNSELING

TWIN CITIES

CONSUMER CREDIT COUNSELING SERVICES OF MINNESOTA, INC.
1111 Third Ave. So., Suite 336
Minneapolis, MN 55404
(612) 349-6953—Minneapolis
(612) 224-2942—St. Paul
(612) 432-8955—Apple Valley

Non-profit financial counseling service for individuals and families. Budget counseling and debt repayment plan which contacts creditors to negotiate reduced payments. Client makes payments to CCCS. Sliding fee.

CONSUMER CREDIT COUNSELING SERVICES, INC.
Family Service of St. Croix

STILLWATER
216 W. Myrtle
Stillwater, MN 55082
(612) 439-4840

WOODBURY
6949 Valley Creek Road
Woodbury, MN 55125
(612) 735-5405

Financial counseling service. Serving east metro and western Wisconsin. Financial assessment, budgeting and debt repayment plans. Crisis intervention for threat of mortgage foreclosure, eviction, utility shut-offs, harassment by creditors. Money management workshops and classes. Mental-health counseling. Sliding fee scale.

FAMILY & CHILDREN'S SERVICE OF THE MINNEAPOLIS METRO AREA
414 So. 8th Street
Minneapolis, MN 55404
(612) 339-9101

Financial counseling service. Assistance with budgeting, money management, debt repayment plans. Client maintains responsibility for making payments directly to creditor. Agency also offers individual and family mental-health counseling. Sliding fee.

FAMILY SERVICE INC.
166 Fourth St. E., Suite 200
St. Paul, MN 55101
(612) 222-0311

Financial counseling service. In-depth assessment of financial situation, budgeting, debt repayment plans. Crisis intervention for threat of mortgage foreclosure, eviction, utility shut-offs or harassment by creditors. Money management workshops and classes. Mental-health counseling available. Sliding fee.

RESOURCES FOR BASIC NEEDS

NORTHERN MINNESOTA

CONSUMER CREDIT COUNSELING SERVICE
LUTHERAN SOCIAL SERVICES
424 W. Superior Street
Duluth, MN 55802
(218) 726-4767

VILLAGE FAMILY SERVICE CENTER
Call for locations in Brainerd, St. Cloud, Alexandria, Detroit Lakes, and Roseau.
(800) 450-4019

Offers budget counseling, debt management, money control workshops, and consumer credit information. Sliding fee.

CENTRAL MINNESOTA

CARITAS FAMILY SERVICES
305 No. 7th Avenue
St. Cloud, MN 56303
(612) 252-4121

Financial counseling service. Offers budget and money management counseling, debt repayment planning, seminars. Advocate in negotiations with creditors. Financial management support group. Free (nominal fee for seminars). Call for appointment.

CONSUMER CREDIT COUNSELING SERVICE
Village Family Service Center

Call for locations in Brainerd, St. Cloud, Alexandria, Detroit Lakes, Roseau.
(800) 450-4019

Offers budget counseling, debt management, money control workshops, consumer credit information. Sliding fee.

This chapter continues on the following page.

MINNESOTA JOB SEEKER'S SOURCEBOOK

SOUTHERN MINNESOTA

CONSUMER CREDIT COUNSELING SERVICES OF ROCHESTER, INC.
Call for office location in Austin.
903 W. Center St., Suite 230
Rochester, MN 55902-6278
(507) 281-6299

Non-profit financial counseling service for individuals and families. Offers budget counseling and debt repayment plan which contacts creditors to negotiate reduced payments. Offices in Rochester and Austin. Client makes payments directly to CCCS. Sliding fee.

WESTERN WISCONSIN

CONSUMER CREDIT COUNSELING SERVICES

HUDSON
Family Service of St. Croix
Second Street Crossing
512 Second Street
Hudson, WI 54016
(715) 386-2066

LA CROSSE
128 So. Sixth Street
La Crosse, WI 54602
(608) 782-0702

Financial counseling service. Serving the east Twin Cities metro area and western Wisconsin. Services include financial assessment, budgeting and debt repayment plans. Crisis intervention for threat of mortgage foreclosure, eviction, utility shut-offs, harassment by creditors. Also offers money management workshops and classes. Mental-health counseling available. Sliding fee scale.

CHAPTER SIX

EMPLOYMENT ALTERNATIVES

Okay, so you're not exactly sure you want to plunge back into the same old job at a brand new company. Maybe you're bored with a dead-end position. Maybe you lost your job during the last corporate cut, and the possibilities of finding another one in your industry look pretty bleak.

Maybe it's time to consider your options.

In this section, you'll encounter alternatives to re-entering the traditional job market: Resources for buying or starting a business, contract and temporary employers, retirement planning assistance. You will also find services to help you explore interim solutions: Career-minded volunteer opportunities, relocation resources and schools and retraining centers.

For those with the luxury of making choices, here's where to look.

Contract & Temporary Employment Services

Here's an astonishing fact: Less than half of all working adults are employed full-time by a single employer. Temporary employment is a $2 billion industry—and growing. Opportunities even exist for temporary managers, executives and professionals.

Temporary employment is an up and coming work alternative. Employment is offered on an assignment basis ranging from one day to six months to several years. For those out of work, temporary employment can provide much-needed interim income, networking opportunities, diversity of assignments, and flexible scheduling.

Temporary work is also a prime opportunity to try out different employers. Likewise, companies use temporary work as a "no-risk" means to try out potential employees. Many of these trial relationships have a happy ending. Forbes magazine reported that about 25 percent of all temp executives are subsequently hired on a permanent basis.

In contrast to temporary employment, often typified by entry level or clerical positions, contract employment is geared to highly trained technical personnel in engineering, computer engineering, technical writing, and other areas. In recent years, contract opportunities have broadened beyond the technical sphere. It is not uncommon today to encounter contract workers in accounting, finance, sales, and management areas. Some contract firms also act as search firms, recruiting for permanent positions.

CONTRACT & TEMPORARY EMPLOYMENT

Some tips for working with temp or contract services: Be selective about which firms or agencies you approach. Clarify the type of work you want, the salary level that's acceptable to you, the days or times you can work, how far you're willing to travel, and the duration of an assignment you're willing to accept. Request a written agreement specifying the details of each assignment.

IMPORTANT: If you're currently receiving unemployment compensation, a contract or temp position could affect your continuing eligibility for these benefits. Likewise, if you complete a temp assignment, then turn down a second assignment, your benefits could be jeopardized. Call the Job Service office where you applied for unemployment. Ask a representative to clarify the guidelines.

The following listings include contract employment services specializing in technical fields, and other professional opportunities. We have also listed only those temporary services located <u>outside</u> of the Twin Cities area. In the Twin Cities, there are hundreds of temp agencies. We could not do justice to them all in our limited space. For that reason we opted to list only three which target older workers. To locate Twin Cities temporary services, please refer to the metro area Yellow Pages.

MINNESOTA JOB SEEKER'S SOURCEBOOK

See also Chapter Four, Search Firms and Employment Agencies, for more organizations that offer contract and permanent employment.

TWIN CITIES

ADVANCE / POSSIS TECHNICAL SERVICES INC.
710 Pennsylvania Ave. So.
Minneapolis, MN 55426
(612) 545-1472   Fax—(612) 545-3493

Contract employment service. Specializes in recruitment of engineering, drafting, design, computer engineering, and technical writing personnel. Mail resume; follow up by phone.

ANDCOR HUMAN RESOURCES
600 U.S. Hwy. 169, Suite 1150
St. Louis Park, MN 55426
(612) 546-0966

Contract employment service. Specializes in permanent and interim placement of professionals in a variety of industries. Opportunities for technical and non-technical personnel in sales and marketing, human resources, and finance. Mail resume; follow up by phone.

CDI CORPORATION — NORTH CENTRAL
5775 Wayzata Blvd., Suite 875
St. Louis Park, MN 55416
(612) 541-9967   Fax—(612) 541-9605

Contract employment service. Specializes in engineering and technical services with positions for engineers, project leaders, electronic technicians, drafters, and designers, computer engineers.

CONTRACT & TEMPORARY EMPLOYMENT

CENTURY DESIGN INC.
530 15th Ave. So.
Hopkins, MN 55343
(612) 935-0033   Fax—(612) 935-4295

Contract employment service. Specializes in positions in all industries for technical writers, editors, illustrators, desktop publishers, instructional designers and developers, and multimedia specialists. Mail resume; follow up by phone.

CONSOLIDATED SERVICES
10125 Crosstown Circle, Suite 230
Eden Prairie, MN 55344
(612) 941-0149   Fax—(612) 941-6983

Contract employment service. Specializes in engineering industry. Positions for drafters, designers, and software engineers. Mail resume; follow up by phone. No fees.

DACON ENGINEERING AND SERVICE COMPANY, INC.
4915 W. 35th Street
Minneapolis, MN 55416
(612) 920-8040   Fax—(612) 920-7619

Contract employment service. Specializes in engineering and technical positions. Mail or fax resume; follow up by phone. No fees.

DASHE & THOMSON TECHNICAL WRITING CONSULTANTS
401 No. Third St., Suite 500
Minneapolis, MN 55401
(612) 338-4911   Fax—(612) 338-4920

Contract employment service. Specializes in positions for Fortune 500 companies. Positions for technical writers, editors, illustrators, and desktop publishers. Mail resume; follow up by phone.

This chapter continues on the following page.

DEVELOPMENT RESOURCE GROUP
2722 Hwy. 694, Suite 230
New Brighton, MN 55112
(612) 636-9141   Fax—(612) 636-9312

Contract employment service. Specializes in electronics industry with focus in biomedical. Positions for hardware/software engineers, technicians, and principal design engineers. Call for information.

DISTINCTION IN DESIGN
14264 23rd Ave. No.
Plymouth, MN 55447
(612) 550-1138   Fax—(612) 550-1349

Contract employment service. Specializes in placement within high-tech engineering and manufacturing companies. Positions for engineers, design drafters, technicians. Mail resume; follow up by phone. No fees.

ENGINEERING RESOURCES OF MINNESOTA
1315 Rice Creek Road
Fridley, MN 55432
(612) 572-0415   Fax—(612) 572-2433

Contract employment service. Specializes in engineering industry. Positions for drafters, programmers, engineers, and technicians. Mail resume; follow up by phone. No fees.

ESP SOFTWARE SERVICES, INC.
701 Fourth Ave. So., Suite 1800
Minneapolis, MN 55415
(612) 337-3000

Contract employment service. Specializes in data processing industry. Opportunities for programmers, analysts, systems programmers, and project leaders. Call for appointment.

CONTRACT & TEMPORARY EMPLOYMENT

FLATLEY SERVICES
3600 W. 80th St., Suite 535
Bloomington, MN 55431
(612) 896-3435

Contract employment service. Diverse contract opportunities for legal, clerical/light industrial, records/storage management, software/data-processing, and engineering project management personnel. Also seeks degreed and non-degreed engineers, designers, CAD operators, drafters, architects, surveyors, para-technical, food processing, engineering, and technical assembly personnel. Mail resume; follow up by phone.

IDI CORPORATION
511 11th Ave. So., Suite 446
Minneapolis, MN 55415
(612) 333-4728   Fax—(612) 333-0141

Contract employment service. Specializes in temporary and some permanent placement of positions in the mechanical engineering industry. Mail resume; follow up by phone. No fees.

KELLY TEMPORARY SERVICES—ENCORE
3033 Campus Drive, Suite 430
Plymouth, MN 55441
(612) 553-1160

Temporary employment service. Specializes in temporary placement of mature workers in various industries. Positions for clerical, marketing, professional, technical, engineering, and accounting personnel. Call for appointment. No fees.

GEORGE KONIK ASSOCIATES, INC.
7242 Metro Blvd.
Minneapolis, MN 55439
(612) 835-5550

Contract employment service. Specializes in all disciplines of engineering industry. Short and long-term assignments for drafters, designers, engineers, programmers, and project engineers. Mail resume; follow up by phone.

NATIONAL ENGINEERING RESOURCES, INC.
P.O. Box 29512
Brooklyn Park, MN 55429
(612) 561-7610   Fax—(612) 561-7675

Contract employment service. Specializes in engineering industry. Positions for designers, engineers, drafters, CAD operators, and quality control personnel. Mail resume; follow up by phone. No fees.

PROGRAMMING ALTERNATIVES INC.
6750 France Ave. So.
Edina, MN 55435
(612) 922-1103   Fax—(612) 922-3726

Contract and permanent placement of experienced data processing and engineering professionals including programmers, analysts, and project leaders. Call for appointment.

RFA/MINNESOTA ENGINEERING
5666 Lincoln Drive
Edina, MN 55436
(612) 935-1761   Fax—(612) 935-1767

Contract employment service. Specializes in contract and permanent positions in engineering design. Positions include detailers, layout, designers, and mechanical engineers. Call for appointment. No fees.

RETIREMENT ENTERPRISES, INC.
33 W. 65th St., Suite 10
Richfield, MN 55423
(612) 869-3301   Fax—(612) 869-8702

Temporary employment service and search firm. Specializes in temporary and permanent placement of mature workers in various industries. Positions for clerical, assembly, accounting, engineering, sales, computer programming. Call for appointment. No fees.

CONTRACT & TEMPORARY EMPLOYMENT

H. L. YOH / SALEM TECHNICAL SERVICES
2626 E. 82nd St., Suite 355
Bloomington, MN 55425
(612) 854-2400   Fax—(612) 854-0512

Contract employment service. Specializes in placement of technically skilled, experienced personnel in engineering, electronics, manufacturing, and architecture. Mail resume; follow up by phone.

SENIOR DESIGN CORPORATION
7600 Parklawn Avenue
Edina, MN 55435
(612) 831-0111   Fax—(612) 831-0494

Contract employment service. Specializes in placement of technical professionals such as engineers, drafters, computer specialists, and office support. Mail resume; follow up by phone.

SOURCE TECH CORPORATION
7600 Parklawn Ave., Suite 204
Edina, MN 55435
(612) 831-8210   Fax—(612) 831-0494

Contract employment service. Specializes in engineering, drafting, technical positions. Mail or fax resume; follow up by phone. No fees.

ST. CROIX TECHNICAL
8300 Norman Center Dr., Suite 890
Bloomington, Mn 55437
(612) 832-8390   Fax—(612) 832-8366

Contract employment service. Specializes in all levels of positions in engineering and manufacturing industries. Positions for programmers, drafters, machine operators, designers, and technicians. Mail or fax resume; follow up by phone. No fees.

This chapter continues on the following page.

STROM ENGINEERING CORPORATION
10505 Wayzata Blvd.
Minnetonka, MN 55305
(612) 544-8644   Fax—(612) 544-2451

Contract engineering service. Specializes in recruitment of engineering, drafting, design, technical writing, and CAD personnel. Locations nationwide. Mail or fax resume; follow up by phone.

SUPERIOR SENIOR SERVICES, INC.
2401-1/2 Central Ave. N.E.
Minneapolis, MN 55418
(612) 789-1616   Fax—(612) 789-0803

Temporary employment service. Specializes in temporary placement of active seniors and mature adults in various industries. Positions in light assembly, clerical, engineering, accounting, and professional services. Three Twin Cities locations. Call for appointment. Fees paid by employer.

TAD TECHNICAL SERVICES CORP.
4820 W. 77th St., Suite 207
Edina, MN 55435
(612) 832-5443   Fax—(612) 832-9865

Contract employment service for technical engineering personnel. Opportunities for software and hardware engineers, programmers, designers, drafters, technical writers, technicians, and quality assurance specialists. Mail resume; follow up by phone.

TECH CENTRAL INC.
7101 York Ave. So.
Edina, MN 55435
(612) 921-3380   Fax—(612) 921-3282

Contract employment service. Specializes in permanent and temporary placement in the engineering industry. Positions for CAD operators, engineers, and architects. Mail resume. No fees.

CONTRACT & TEMPORARY EMPLOYMENT

TECHNIFORCE
10800 Lyndale Ave. So., Suite 165
Bloomington, MN 55420
(612) 881-6499   Fax—(612) 881-6295

Contract employment service. Specializes in engineering industry with positions for drafters and technicians. Mail or fax resume; follow up by phone. No fees.

TECHPOWER, INC.
4510 W. 77th Street
Edina, MN 55435
(612) 831-7444   Fax—(612) 831-8621

Contract employment service. Specializes in engineering and telecommunications industries. Positions for project engineers and programmers. Mail or fax resume; follow up by phone. No fees.

THE NYCOR GROUP
4930 W. 77th St., Suite 300
Minneapolis, MN 55435
(612) 831-6444   Fax—(612) 835-2883

Contract employment and executive search in all engineering disciplines. Specializes in placement of electrical, computer, biomedical, environmental, civil, mechanical, and chemical engineering personnel. Mail resume; follow up by phone. Fees paid by employer.

WESTERN TECHNICAL SERVICES
3601 Minnesota Dr., Suite 500
Bloomington, MN 55435
(612) 835-4743   Fax—(612) 835-5419

Contract employment service. Specializes in temporary and contract placement in a variety of industries. Positions for technicians, designers, drafters, and programmers. Mail or fax resume; follow up by phone. No fees.

This chapter continues on the following page.

MINNESOTA JOB SEEKER'S SOURCEBOOK

NORTHERN MINNESOTA

MANPOWER TEMPORARY SERVICES
516 First Bank Place
Duluth, MN 55802
(218) 727-8891   Fax—(218) 727-8725

Temporary employment service. Specializes in entry-level positions in various fields. Call for appointment. No fees.

NORTHSTAR PERSONNEL

720 Paul Bunyon Drive
Bemidji, MN 56601
(218) 751-9690

220 N.W. First Avenue
Grand Rapids, MN 55744
(218) 327-1133

522 E. Howard Street
Hibbing, MN 55746
(218) 262-3478

Employment agency. Temporary and contract opportunities in various fields and levels. Call for appointment. Fees paid by employer.

SEARCH RESOURCES, INC.
214 First Ave. N.W.
Grand Rapids, MN 55744
(218) 326-9461   Fax—(218) 326-9463

Temporary, contract, and permanent placements in manufacturing industry. Call for appointment. Fees paid by employer.

CENTRAL MINNESOTA

ACTION-PLUS TEMPORARY SERVICE, INC.
141 E. Broadway
Monticello, MN 55362
(612) 295-4005   Fax—(612) 295-6240

Temporary employment service. Entry-level positions in manufacturing, food production, and other industries. Call for appointment. No fees.

CONTRACT & TEMPORARY EMPLOYMENT

DOBBS PRO STAFF
26 Sixth Ave. No., Suite 103
St. Cloud, MN 56302
(612) 656-9777

Temporary employment service. Positions in general clerical and light industrial. Call for appointment. Fees paid by employer.

EXPRESS PERSONNEL SERVICES
606 So. 25th Ave., Suite 104
St. Cloud, MN 56301
(612) 251-1038

Temporary employment in light industrial, clerical, and medical. Training may be available. Call or drop in. Fees paid by employer.

KELLY TEMPORARY SERVICES
1010 W. St. Germain, Suite 400
St. Cloud, MN 56301
(612) 253-7430   (800) 447-6447

Temporary employment in light industrial, secretarial, sales promotion, data entry. Call for appointment. Fees paid by employer.

MANPOWER TEMPORARY SERVICES
3400 No. First St., Suite 101
St. Cloud, MN 56303
(612) 251-1924

Temporary employment in industrial, data entry, word processing, technical. Computer training. Fees paid by employer.

QUALITY TEMP
15 No. Sixth Ave., Suite D
St. Cloud, MN 56303
(612) 259-4004

Temporary employment service. Long-term temporary assignments in light industrial positions. Call for appointment. Fees paid by employer.

THE WORK CONNECTION
14 7th Ave. No.
St. Cloud, MN 56301
(612) 259-9675

Temporary employment service. General, industrial, and clerical positions for entry through senior-level personnel. Drop in to complete an application. Applications kept on file one year. Fees paid by employer.

SOUTHERN MINNESOTA

GIBBS TEMPORARY EMPLOYMENT SERVICE
1915 Hwy. 52 No., Suite 222-C
Rochester, MN 55901
(507) 288-3623   Fax—(507) 288-6586

Temporary employment service. Specializes in entry level positions in variety of industries. Call for appointment. No fees.

KELLY TEMPORARY SERVICES
3800 Hwy. 52 No., Suite 130
Rochester, MN 55901
(507) 282-1584   (800) 448-8908

Temporary employment service. Specializes in positions at all levels in manufacturing, health care, medical. Call for appointment. No fees.

MANPOWER TEMPORARY SERVICES
920 Hoffman Drive   940 37th St. N.W.
Owatonna, MN 55060   Rochester, MN 55901
(507) 451-3404   (800) 638-9889 (507) 285-0710

Temporary employment service. Specializes in positions at all levels in variety of industries. Call for appointment. No fees.

CONTRACT & TEMPORARY EMPLOYMENT

QUALITY TEMP
147 W. Bridge Street
Owatonna, MN 55060
(507) 455-9242

1600 Madison Ave., Suite 108
Mankato, MN 56001
(507) 387-5009

1915 Hwy. 52 No., Suite 102
Rochester, MN 55901
(507) 285-5343

Temporary employment service. Specializes in entry level and production personnel in manufacturing industry. Call for appointment. No fees.

TECHNICAL CAREER PLACEMENTS INC.
1915 Highway 52 No., Suite 222-C
Rochester, MN 55901
(507) 288-3623   Fax—(507) 288-6586

Contract/permanent employment service. Placements of mid- to upper management for engineers, hardware/software engineers, and computer programmers. Mail or fax resume. Generally fees paid by employer.

WESTERN WISCONSIN

MANPOWER TEMPORARY SERVICES
1800 Hwy. 16, Suite D
La Crosse, WI 54601
(608) 781-8899   Fax—(608) 781-8897

Temporary employment service. Specializes in entry level positions in various fields. Call for appointment. No fees.

THE WORK CONNECTION
1045 W. Clairemont
Eau Claire, WI 54701
(715) 836-9675   (715) 836-7979

Temporary and permanent employment service. Specializes in all levels of positions in various industries. Call for appointment. No fees.

Resources For Buying or Starting A Business

Unemployment produces entrepreneurs. At least that's what recent data by the Department of Labor reveals. One year after the last recession began in July of 1990, ranks of self-employed swelled to the highest level in 25 years. Some job search consultants report that one in six of their clients goes solo after losing a job.

No surprise.

To the victims of corporate downsizing or government cutbacks, business ownership promises perks: Control. Income potential. Challenge. Independence. Flexible hours. To name a few.

So, if you want your next boss to be *you*, your first job as CEO is to approach the task armed with as much information as possible.

Minnesota and Wisconsin offer a surprising array of resources to would-be entrepreneurs about how to launch a new enterprise or buy an existing one. Many of these services are free or low cost. Some offer start-up kits, guides or business consulting services. Others provide opportunities for networking through workshops, seminars, and entrepreneurial associations. There are even mentorship programs staffed by current or retired business owners familiar with specific businesses or industries.

SELF EMPLOYMENT RESOURCES

Libraries can help you track down potential competition or research an industry. Colleges, technical schools, and community education departments also offer small business education.

Buyers of businesses must creatively investigate resources. Healthy businesses are not always publicly announced for sale. To seek out leads, consult business brokers or newspaper ads. Contact bankers, attorneys, accountants, sales reps, insurance agents, SBA liquidation officers and trade association staff.

In addition to the resources found on the following pages, several business "incubator" centers are listed below that may provide office, warehouse or retail space at below-market rent, flexible leases, shared office services, and free business advice.

BUSINESS INCUBATORS
TWIN CITIES

The Franklin Business Center, Minneapolis, (612) 870-7555
University Technology Center, Minneapolis, (612) 379-3800
Empire Builder Center, St. Paul, (612) 223-8600.
Genesis Business Centers LTD, Blaine, (612) 780-6321
University of St. Thomas Enterprise Center, Chaska, (612) 448-8800.

BUSINESS INCUBATORS
GREATER MINNESOTA

Aitkin County Growth Center, Aitkin, (218) 927-2172.
Breckenridge Business Center, Breckenridge, (218) 643-1173.
Cannon Business Industrial Center, Cannon Falls, (507) 263-3954
Fairmont Business Development Center, Fairmont, (507) 238-9461.
Henderson Business Center, Henderson, (612) 248-9664.
Leech Lake Retail Center, Cass Lake, (218) 335-8217.
Mankato Manufacturing Incubator, Mankato, (507) 387-8686.
Owatonna Incubator Inc., Owatonna, (507) 451-0517.

MINNESOTA

MINNESOTA ENTREPRENEURS' CLUB
University of St. Thomas, MPL 100
1000 LaSalle Avenue
Minneapolis, MN 55403
(612) 897-5072

This networking organization provides support to new and experienced entrepreneurs. Monthly meetings feature well-known speakers. Annual membership, $35; Non-members, $10 per meeting.

MINNESOTA PROJECT OUTREACH
Minnesota Technology, Inc.
The Mill Place, Suite 400
111 Third Ave. So.
Minneapolis, MN 55401
(612) 851-7750—Twin Cities
(800) 338-7005—Greater Minnesota

Business assistance program. Comprehensive service assisting state businesses with technology and scientific information available from University of Minnesota and other institutions. Also assists small and mid-sized businesses in finding technical and financial assistance. Provides referrals to state and national consultants, conducts business research, and vendor/patent searches. Call for Minnesota locations.

MINNESOTA SMALL BUSINESS DEVELOPMENT CENTERS
Call for locations throughout Minnesota.
(612) 223-8663—Twin Cities only
(800) 657-3858—Greater Minnesota only

Business assistance program for experienced or new entrepreneurs. Offices located throughout Minnesota, are generally housed on college campuses. Services include one-to-one consulting on business plans, accounting, marketing, financing and operations management. Also offers workshops and seminars on specialized topics. Free.

SELF EMPLOYMENT RESOURCES

NATIONAL ASSOCIATION FOR THE SELF-EMPLOYED
7800 Metro Parkway, Suite 103
Bloomington, MN 55425
(612) 854-1416   (800) 466-6273

Offers group discounts on business and personal products and services. Bimonthly newspaper. Toll-free access to small business consultants and free business start-up publications. Call for information. Dues are $72/year.

REGIONAL BUSINESS PUBLICATIONS

There are several regional business publications designed to assist new and existing business owners. Most can be found in libraries or on local newsstands. To subscribe, call the numbers listed below.

- CityBusiness   (612) 591-2531
- Corporate Report Minnesota   (612) 591-2531
- Twin Cities Business Monthly   (612) 339-7571
- Minnesota Business Opportunities   (612) 844-0400
- Minnesota Ventures   (612) 338-3828
- Homebased & Small Business Network   (612) 689-1630

SBA SMALL BUSINESS ANSWER DESK
U.S. Small Business Administration
(800) 827-5722

Business assistance helpline. Pre-recorded information on how to start a business and order SBA publications. Also offers option to speak directly to SBA counselor.

THE COLLABORATIVE
10 So. Fifth St., Suite 415
Minneapolis, MN 55402
(612) 338-3828   Fax—(612) 338-1876

Information and networking for growing Minnesota companies. Provides meetings, workshops, conferences, and publications. Membership, $295—595.

MINNESOTA JOB SEEKER'S SOURCEBOOK

U.S. SMALL BUSINESS ADMINISTRATION
610-C Butler Square, 100 No. 6th Street
Minneapolis, MN 55403
(612) 370-2324

Business assistance program. Free Start-Up Kit includes basic steps for starting a small business, helpful phone numbers, sample business plan outline, and financial information. Call or write for information.

TWIN CITIES

METROPOLITAN ECONOMIC DEVELOPMENT ASSO.
2021 E. Hennepin Ave., Suite 370
Minneapolis, MN 55413
(612) 378-0361

Open to African-Americans, Hispanics, Asians, Native Americans, and other minorities. Offers business consulting, mentorship program, seminars. Call for appointment. Consulting is free.

SCORE
Service Corps of Retired Executives

MINNEAPOLIS
5217 Wayzata Blvd.
St. Louis Park, MN 55416
(612) 591-0539

ST. PAUL
101 Norwest Center, 55 E. Fifth St.
St. Paul, MN 55101
(612) 223-5010

Business assistance program. Sponsors seminars covering SBA loan applications, financial statements, marketing plans, market research. Free counseling by retired business people. Small fee for seminars.

WOMENVENTURE
2324 University Ave. W., Suite 200
St. Paul, MN 55114
(612) 646-3808

Business assistance program for women. Help with business plans, cash flow, marketing, loans, record-keeping. Seminars, business plan kit, and "last resort" small loan fund. Sliding fee.

SELF EMPLOYMENT RESOURCES

NORTHERN MINNESOTA

ARROWHEAD COMMUNITY ECONOMIC ASSISTANCE CORP. (ACEAC)
702 Third Ave. South
Virginia, MN 55792-2797
(800) 662-5711

Small business center helps with business plans, loan applications, operations management. Also offers workshops and counseling.

NORTHEAST ENTREPRENEUR FUND, INC.
140 Olcott Plaza
Virginia, MN 55792
(218) 749-4191   Fax—(218) 741-4249

Offers workshops, business counseling. loan program for startup and experienced business owners in Aitkin, Carlton, Cook, Itasca, Lake, St. Louis and Koochiching Counties. Call for information. Sliding Fee.

REGIONAL DEVELOPMENT COMMISSIONS

ARROWHEAD
330 Canal Park Drive
Duluth, MN 55802
(218) 722-5545   (800) 232-0707

HEADWATERS
403 Fourth St. N.W., Suite 310
Bemidji, MN 56601
(218) 751-3108

NORTHWEST
525 Brooks Avenue
Thief River Falls, MN 56701
(218) 681-2637   Fax—(218) 681-2670

Small business assistance center offering workshops, publications, networking opportunities. Revolving loan fund for startup and experienced business owners. Call for appointment. Free.

This chapter continues on the following page.

TRI-COUNTY COMMUNITY ACTION PROGRAM
2410 Oak Street
Brainerd, MN 56401
(218) 829-2410   Fax—(218) 829-0494

Small business assistance for startup or experienced business owners in Crow Wing, Morrison, and Todd Counties who meet income requirements. Offers workshops/seminars on business plans, marketing, record-keeping; counseling for completing loan applications. Call for appointment. Free to eligible individuals.

CENTRAL MINNESOTA

REGIONAL DEVELOPMENT COMMISSIONS

CENTRAL
611 Iowa Avenue
Staples, MN 56479
(218) 894-3233

MID-MINNESOTA
333 W. 6th Street
Willmar, MN 56201
(612) 235-8504

Small business assistance center offers workshops, publications, networking opportunities, revolving loan fund for startup and experienced business owners. Call for appointment. Free.

ST. CLOUD AREA ECONOMIC DEVELOPMENT PARTNERSHIP

ST. CLOUD CHAMBER OF COMMERCE
30 Sixth Ave. South
St. Cloud, MN 56302
(612) 252-2177   (612) 251-2940

Publishes "Getting Started in Business in the St. Cloud Area" listing financing options, marketing and promotion resources, and vendors. Also includes Business Start-Up check list and a sample business plan. Available from Chamber for $5.

SELF EMPLOYMENT RESOURCES

SCORE
Service Corps of Retired Executives

ALEXANDRIA
Alexandria Technical College
1601 Jefferson Street
Alexandria, MN 56308
(612) 762-4502

ORTONVILLE
Ortonville Economic Dvelopment
315 Madison Avenue
Ortonville, MN 56278
(612) 839-2618

ST. CLOUD
Norwest Bank Building
400 Second St. So., Suite 430
St. Cloud, MN 56301
(612) 255-4955

Business assistance program. Sponsors seminars covering SBA loan applications, financial statements, marketing plans, business structure, market research. Free individual counseling by retired business people to new and experienced business owners. Small fee for seminars.

TRI-COUNTY COMMUNITY ACTION PROGRAM
501 Le Mieur Street
P.O. Box 368
Little Falls, MN 56345
(612) 632-3691   Fax—(612) 632-3695

For business owners in Crow Wing, Morrison, and Todd Counties who meet income requirements. Offers workshops on business plans, marketing, record-keeping, loan applications. Free.

SOUTHERN MINNESOTA

DAY WORKS
120 N.E. First Street
Rochester, MN 55906
(507) 281-6323   Fax—(507) 281-6605

Short-term office rentals. Services include receptionist, phones, copier, computer and fax. Fees, $15/hour; $55/day; $225/week.

MINNESOTA JOB SEEKER'S SOURCEBOOK

REGIONAL DEVELOPMENT COMMISSIONS

REGION 9
P.O. Box 3367
Mankato, MN 56002
(507) 387-5643   (800) 450-5643

SOUTHWEST
2524 Broadway Avenue
Slayton, MN 56172
(507) 836-8547

Small business assistance center. Workshops, revolving loan fund for startup and experienced business owners. Call for appointment. Free.

SCORE
Service Corps of Retired Executives

Business assistance program. Seminars cover SBA loan applications, financial statements, marketing plans, market research. Free counseling by retired business people. Small fee for seminars.

ALBERT LEA
202 No. Broadway
Albert Lea, MN 56007
(507) 373-3939

OWATONNA
320 Hoffman Drive
Owatonna, MN 55060
(507) 451-7970

AUSTIN
300 No. Main Street
Austin, MN 55912
(507) 437-4561

RED WING
308 Pioneer Road
Red Wing, MN 55066
(612) 388-4079

FAIRMONT
206 No. State Street
Fairmont, MN 56031
(507) 235-5547

ROCHESTER
220 So. Broadway, Suite 100
Rochester, MN 55904
(507) 288-1122

MANKATO
107 Riverfront Drive
Mankato, MN 56001
(507) 345-4519

WINONA
67 Main Street
Winona, MN 55987
(507) 452-2272

MARSHALL
501 West Main
Marshall, MN 56258
(507) 532-4484

WORTHINGTON
1018 Fourth Avenue
Worthington, MN 56187
(507) 372-2919

SELF EMPLOYMENT RESOURCES

SOUTHEASTERN MINNESOTA INITIATIVE FUND
P.O. Box 570
Owatonna, MN 55060
(507) 455-3215   Fax—(507) 455-2098

Networking group and funding source. Open to startup and experienced business owners. Offers workshops, seminars, assistance with loan applications. Call or write for free publications.

WESTERN WISCONSIN

BUSINESS INCUBATION CENTER
2231 Catlin Ave., Suite 400
Superior, WI 54880
(715) 394-7388   Fax—(715) 394-7414

Assistance with business plans, loan applications, marketing, cash-flow management. Workshops, counseling, access to low-cost office space. Call for appointment and fees.

SCORE
Service Corps of Retired Executives

EAU CLAIRE
510 So. Barstow
Eau Claire, WI 54701
(715) 834-1573

LA CROSSE
712 Main Street
La Crosse, WI 54601
(608) 784-4880

Business assistance program. Sponsors "Going-into-Business" seminars covering SBA loan applications, financial statements, marketing plan, business structure, market research. Free individual counseling by retired business people and professionals to new and experienced business owners. Call to receive Request for Counseling form. Small fee for seminars.

Career-Minded Volunteering

Volunteer work can offer job seekers an interesting range of experience and opportunities. Even though it's not "for pay," a volunteer job can help you:

- Stay professionally active
- Learn new career skills
- Enhance your resume
- Expand your network of contacts
- Earn a letter of recommendation
- Add structure to your work week
- Introduce you to an organization you'd like to target for a paying job down the road.

In 1976, Congress passed a resolution urging all public and private businesses to recognize volunteer experience in their hiring practices. And for good reason. Volunteers contribute an impressive spectrum of talent and professionalism to an organization.

Increasingly, volunteers are demanding more out of their volunteer work than just a feel-good experience. In response, many organizations have upgraded responsibilities. It is not uncommon to find volunteers working in marketing, accounting, public relations, computer, or other professional areas. Some organizations also provide formal classroom instruction or on-the-job training.

If career enhancement is high on your agenda, there are literally hundreds of organizations and agencies to choose from. But choose your volunteer work carefully. Select a job where you can apply your skills and talents; you don't want to fold and collate if you have a CPA degree or 20 years in marketing.

CAREER-MINDED VOLUNTEER OPPORTUNITIES

The first place to start researching volunteer opportunities is with one of the numerous clearinghouse referral agencies. Most will match your interests and experience with an appropriate organization, usually non-profit or government. Tell the referral agency what you want to do, what you can do, what you want to learn, where you want to work, etc. They will provide you with several choices.

A few tips: Be sure to choose an opportunity that will broaden your horizons and/or complement your resume. Document your duties and your accomplishments. Ask for increased responsibilities as the situation arises. And don't forget to tell prospective employers about this valuable experience.

Listed below are the major volunteer referral services in Minnesota and western Wisconsin.

TWIN CITIES

COMMUNITY VOLUNTEER SERVICE OF ST. CROIX VALLEY AREA
1965 So. Greeley
Stillwater, MN 55082
(612) 439-7434

Volunteer opportunities in Washington County in human services, computers, teaching, PR, graphic design, income tax preparation, etc. Hours, time commitment, and training vary. Call for information.

UNITED WAY'S VOLUNTEER CENTER
404 So. 8th Street
Minneapolis, MN 55404
(612) 340-7621

Volunteer referral service with 5,000 volunteer opportunities at non-profit agencies, schools and government in west metro, in PR, healthcare, computer services, accounting, marketing, graphic design. Time commitment, training, and hours vary. Call for referrals.

VOLUNTARY ACTION CENTER OF THE ST. PAUL AREA, INC.
251 Starkey St., Suite 127
St. Paul, MN 55107-1821
(612) 227-3938

Volunteer referral service serving Ramsey, Washington, and Dakota Counties. Opportunities with schools, non-profit organizations, government. Database of 4,000 positions. Skills needed in human/social services, computers, public relations, fundraising, graphic design, cultural arts, marketing, secretarial. Time commitment, training, and scheduling is individualized with each agency. Position may provide on-the-job training, letters of recommendation. Call for information.

GREATER MINNESOTA

HIBBING VOLUNTEER COUNCIL
3230 Eighth Ave. East
Hibbing, MN 55746
(218) 262-4784

Volunteer referral service serving northern St. Louis County with volunteer opportunities with non-profit organizations. Database of 150 positions. Skills needed in PR, fundraising. Time commitment, training, and scheduling vary. Volunteer positions may provide training, letters of recommendation. Call for information.

NORTHLAND VOLUNTEER COUNCIL, INC.
Pioneer Building, Room 9
901 Ninth St. No.
Virginia, MN 55734
(218) 749-2227

Volunteer referral service with opportunities with local schools, non-profit organizations, government. Database of 100 current positions in human services, computer, PR, fundraising, graphic design, marketing, and more. Time commitment varies. Positions may provide training and academic credit. Write for information.

THE VOLUNTEER CONNECTION, INC.
903 West Center St., Suite 200
Rochester, MN 55902
(507) 287-2244

Volunteer referral service serving Olmstead County. Database of 400 positions in human services, PR, fundraising. Time commitment, training, scheduling individualized by agency. May receive training, academic credit, letters of recommendation. Call for information.

UNITED WAY OF ST. CLOUD AREA
26 No. 6th Ave., Suite 20
St. Cloud, MN 56303
(612) 252-0227

Volunteer referral service serving Stearns, Benton, and Sherburne Counties. Database of 500 positions. Volunteers also needed with four-year degrees. Time commitment, training is individualized by agency. May provide training, letters of recommendation. Call for interview.

VOLUNTARY ACTION CENTER
925 County Home Road
Grand Rapids, MN 55744
(218) 327-1634

Volunteer referral service serving Itasca County. Database of about 50 current positions. Skills needed in human services, computers, and fundraising. Time commitment varies by assignment. Provides on-the-job training, letters of recommendation. Call for information.

VOLUNTARY ACTION CENTER OF UNITED WAY
424 W. Superior St., Suite 402
Duluth, MN 55802
(218) 726-4776

Volunteer referral service. Serving greater Duluth area. Database of approximately 100 current positions. Skills needed in human services, computer, and graphic design. Time commitment varies by assignment. Provides on-the-job-training, letters of recommendation. Call for information.

VOLUNTEER SERVICES OF CARLTON COUNTY
1003 Cloquet Ave., Rm 102
Cloquet, MN 55720
(218) 879-9238

Volunteer referral service serving Carlton County. Database of 10—15 current positions in human services and computer services. Time commitment varies by assignment. Offers training, academic credit, letters of recommendation. Drop in.

VOLUNTEERS WORKING TOGETHER
418 No. Jefferson, Room 203
Wadena, MN 56482
(218) 631-3510 ext. 321

Volunteer referral service serving Wadena County with approximately 100 positions per year. Skills needed in human services. Time commitment varies by assignment. May offer letters of recommendation, free training. Call for information.

WESTERN WISCONSIN

LUTHERAN HOSPITAL
Volunteer Services
1910 South Avenue
La Crosse, WI 54601
(608) 785-0530

Serving 19 counties in Wisconsin, southeastern Minnesota, northwestern Iowa. Volunteer opportunities with hospitals. Database of approximately 1,000 current positions. Many skills needed including professional skills in human services, computer, PR, fundraising, graphic design, marketing. Flexible time commitment. Volunteer positions may provide on-the-job training, academic credit, letters of recommendation, leadership skills development. Call for information.

Relocation Resources

When a job move means packing up the Chevy for a trek to a new town, your stress-level barometer can hit a high note. Fortunately, there are many services that can help you weather the task.

Before you commit to relocating, carefully weigh the costs and benefits. Put pen to paper and figure out the bottom-line cost of the move. If you've received a job offer, clarify with the prospective employer exactly what relocation benefits or reimbursements apply. Ask your tax specialist about which moving expenses you may be able to deduct on your tax return—and the documentation or records you need to keep.

Call a family meeting and discuss this transition with your spouse and children. How will the move effect them? What about the effect on friends, relatives, or aging parents you may be leaving behind?

Learn about the quality of life in the prospective community. How do the schools rank? What about taxes? The cost of living? Job growth? Commuting distances? Housing costs? Crime rate? Shopping and recreational activities?

For those planning to relocate to or from Minnesota and Wisconsin, these resources can help ease the way:

MINNESOTA

ENROLLMENT OPTIONS HOTLINE
Minnesota Department of Education

(612) 296-1261   (800) 657-3990

Information about how to approach the process of selecting a school in Minnesota. Also provides referrals to publications to help assess Twin Cities and greater Minnesota school districts.

TWIN CITIES

AFFORDABLE HOUSING HOTLINE
The Connection

(612) 922-9000

Twenty-four hour telephone helpline provides callers with listings for Twin Cities rental properties based on caller's needs. Also provides information about Section 8 and subsidized housing. Properties are not pre-screened. Information is provided by property owners. Free.

BURNET RELOCATION MANAGEMENT
Burnet Realty

7550 France Ave. So.
Edina, MN 55435
(612) 844-6500   (800) 388-8700

Real estate agency offers free packet of housing and community information about Twin Cities and other communities in Minnesota and western Wisconsin. Resources describe local attractions, schools, maps, property and income taxes, community profiles. Also offers in-office housing consultation and community orientation. Call for information.

RELOCATION RESOURCES

CHILD CARE RESOURCE AND REFERRAL LINES
(612) 783-4884—Anoka County
(612) 496-2321—Carver/Scott Counties
(612) 431-7752—Dakota County
(612) 341-2066—Hennepin County
(612) 641-0332—Ramsey County
(612) 430-6488—Washington County

Referral helpline. Conducts customized searches for child care based on client's criteria. Call for information. Fees may apply.

EDINA REALTY RELOCATION SERVICES
1400 So. Highway 100, Suite 200
Minneapolis, MN 55416
(612) 591-6400   (800) 328-4344

Real estate agency. Provides extensive free relocation packet with information on Twin Cities housing, community profiles, shopping, maps, attractions, schools, taxes, major employers, search firms. Also provides rental assistance and computerized information comparing departure city with destination city for affordability of housing. Call for information.

GREATER MINNEAPOLIS CHAMBER OF COMMERCE
81 So. 9th Street, Suite 200
Minneapolis, MN 55402-3223
(612) 370-9111—Business Source Order Line

Provides variety of relocation publications to newcomers at a fee with information on housing, schools, income taxes, parks and recreation, community profiles, and more. Career Kit provides regional job-search resources such as major Twin Cities employers, Minnesota salary survey, community profiles, and other helpful publications. Call or write for ordering information.

This chapter continues on the following page.

MINNESOTA JOB SEEKER'S SOURCEBOOK

METROPOLITAN COUNCIL DATA CENTER
Mears Park Centre
230 E. Fifth Street
St. Paul, MN 55101
(612) 291-8140

Extensive information about the greater metropolitan area with census data, maps, housing reports, and economic profiles. Call or write to receive publications directory. Publications sold at modest fees.

RENTAL GUIDES

Apartment Search
2756 Hennepin Ave. So.
Minneapolis, MN 55408
(612) 870-0525   (800) 832-7476

Free apartment locater service with computerized database of Twin Cities rentals. Call for information.

Living Guide
8100 Penn Ave. So., Suite 100
Bloomington, MN 55431
(612) 884-2980

Free guide to Twin Cities rental properties. Published three times a year. Call or write for information.

Start Renting
123 No. Third Street, Suite 508
Minneapolis, MN 55401
(612) 340-9900

Free bi-weekly guide to Twin Cities rental properties. Call or write for information.

RELOCATION RESOURCES

SAINT PAUL AREA CHAMBER OF COMMERCE
101 Norwest Center
55 East Fifth Street
St. Paul, MN 55101
(612) 223-5000

Provides relocation publications to newcomers at a fee with information on schools, local government, hospitals, taxes, rent sampler, crime statistics, community profiles, major employers, rental information, and more. Call or write for ordering information.

STAR TRIBUNE FAX SERVICE
(612) 525-3555

The Star Tribune daily Twin Cities newspaper provides reprints of past Homes section articles by fax at a fee. Article topics cover choosing a neighborhood and deciding whether to rent or buy. Call for recorded ordering instructions. Touch-tone phone required.

STAR TRIBUNE FONAHOME
6228 Bury Drive
Eden Prairie, MN 55346-1718
(612) 673-8888   (800) 362-4663

Free relocation service provides information on Minnesota housing, day care, schools, local attractions, trailing spouse assistance, and more. Free rental housing information and videotapes about properties in the greater metro area. Also offers referrals to out-of-state relocation resources. Call for information.

TWIN CITIES TOURISM INFORMATION LINE
Greater Minneapolis Chamber of Commerce
(612) 370-9103

Recorded message describes wide variety of Twin Cities attractions, lodging, restaurants, shopping, current events, sporting events, and transportation.

This chapter continues on the following page.

MINNESOTA JOB SEEKER'S SOURCEBOOK

CHAMBERS OF COMMERCE

Call or write area Chambers to request a relocation packet that includes a variety of local community information.

GREATER MINNESOTA

BEMIDJI CHAMBER
300 Bemidji
P.O. Box 850
Bemidji, MN 56601
(800) 458-2223

DULUTH CHAMBER
118 E. Superior Street
Duluth, MN 55802
(218) 722-5501

FARIBAULT CHAMBER
530 Wilson Avenue
P.O. Box 434
Faribault, MN 55021
(507) 334-4381   (800) 658-2354

GRAND RAPIDS CHAMBER
One N.W. Third Street
Grand Rapids, MN 55744
(218) 326-6619   (800) 472-6366

HIBBING CHAMBER
211 E. Howard Street
P.O. Box 727
Hibbing, MN 55746
(218) 262-3895

INTERNATIONAL FALLS CHAMBER
200 Fourth Street
P.O. Box 169
International Falls, MN 56649
(218) 283-9400   (800) 325-5766

MANKATO CHAMBER
220 E. Main
Mankato, MN 56001
(507) 345-4519

MOORHEAD CHAMBER
725 Center Avenue
Moorhead, MN 56560
(218) 236-6200

OWATONNA CHAMBER
320 Hoffman Drive
Owatonna, MN 55060
(507) 451-7970   (800) 423-6466

ROCHESTER CHAMBER
220 So. Broadway, Suite 100
Rochester, MN 55904
(507) 288-1122

ST. CLOUD CHAMBER
P.O. Box 487
St. Cloud, MN 56302
(612) 251-2940

RELOCATION RESOURCES

WESTERN WISCONSIN

EAU CLAIRE
505 So. Dewey, Suite 101
Eau Claire, WI 54701
(715) 834-1204   (800) 944-2449

LA CROSSE
712 Main Street
La Crosse, WI 54601
(608) 784-4880

MENOMONIE
533 No. Broadway
P.O. Box 246
Menomonie, WI 54751
(715) 235-9087   (800) 283-1862

SUPERIOR
305 E. Second Street
Superior, WI 54880
(715) 394-7716   (800) 942-5313

Retirement Planning Services

Ever since you filled out your first job application, you've probably fantasized about retirement. Who doesn't dream about trading in rush-hour commutes for a second cup of morning coffee? Or, exchanging deadlines and DayTimers for long, lazy summers at the cabin?

If you're age 50 or 60-something, and recently out of a job, retirement may be a viable—and enticing—strategy. Even if you are currently employed, but your employer has presented a tempting early retirement incentive, the offer may seem too good to refuse.

But here's the catch: Retirement planning is serious business. Experts say that without good planning, you could face many future years with a short-fall of income.

The watchword? Look before you leap. Ask serious questions. And get expert advice.

There are many types of professionals to turn to for answers. Financial planners. Tax accountants. And attorneys, to name a few. Many local community education departments also offer classes on retirement planning.

With limited space, we couldn't list all of the qualified retirement planning experts in the private sector. Instead, we've opted to include these three non-profit resources that can offer free or low-cost services to help you make savvy retirement decisions.

RETIREMENT PLANNING SERVICES

AARP
American Association of Retired Persons
Publications Fulfillment
601 E Street N.W.
Washington, DC 20077-1214
(202) 434-2277

National association for members, ages 50 and up. Publishes retirement planning and job-seeking materials including: "Look Before You Leap: A Guide to Early Retirement Incentive Programs," "How to Stay Employable, for Mid-Life and Older Workers," "Single Person's Guide to Retirement Planning," and "Working Options—How to Plan Your Job Search and Work Life," plus dozens more. Call or write for a publications directory. Single copies are free.

CENTER FOR CAREER CHANGE
Minnesota Senior Federation
1885 University Ave. S., Suite 190
St. Paul, MN 55104
(612) 645-0261

Open to the public. Offers full range of retirement planning and counseling services. Provides individualized assistance with pension and retirement issues, including legal and technical assistance. Call for information. Fees, $35 per session.

CENTER FOR SENIOR CITIZEN'S EDUCATION
University of St. Thomas
5115 Summit Avenue
St. Paul, MN 55105
(612) 962-5180

Open to the public and targeted to individuals, ages 55 and up. Services include individualized retirement counseling and financial planning provided by professionals with diverse expertise in law, insurance, finance, etc. Also offers university classes, free to qualified participants. Call for information. Services are free.

Schools & Training Centers

Going back to school—business, academic, technical or vocational— is a feasible option for some career plans.

If you're considering a career change, or if you're currently between jobs, enrolling in a class or full-time education program can sharpen your marketability or recharge dated skills. Short-term programs may even provide you with backup or interim training that will help you earn a living during transitional periods of your life.

Most schools that cater to adult students recognize that balancing family, work and school must be as uncomplicated as possible. Therefore, many offer flexible scheduling (day, evening, summer and weekend programs) to earn degrees, diploma's or certificates even if you're working or return to work.

Community and technical colleges in Minnesota and western Wisconsin are listed beginning on page 265.

TWIN CITIES

ACADEMY EDUCATION CENTER
3050 Metro Drive, Suite 200
Minneapolis, MN 55425
(612) 851-0066

Offers certificate and two-year degree programs in accounting, aviation, and computers.

SCHOOLS & TRAINING CENTERS

AUGSBURG COLLEGE
731 21st Ave. So.
Minneapolis, MN 55454
(612) 330-1001

Four-year private liberal arts college. Day and weekend programs.

COLLEGE OF ASSOCIATED ARTS
344 Summit Avenue
St. Paul, MN 55102
(612) 224-3416

Four-year private visual arts college. BFA degrees in communication design, illustration, painting, drawing, printmaking, and sculpture. Full-time day program.

COLLEGE OF ST. CATHERINE
2004 Randolph Avenue
St. Paul, MN 55105
(612) 690-6505   Fax—(612) 690-6024

Academic school. Four-year private liberal arts college for women. Day, evening, weekend, and summer classes. Graduate programs.

CONCORDIA COLLEGE
275 North Syndicate Street
St. Paul, MN 55104
(612) 641-8230

Four-year private liberal arts college offers flexible full and part-time schedules.

DUNWOODY INSTITUTE
818 Dunwoody Blvd.
Minneapolis, MN 55403-1192
(612) 374-5800

Technical vocational school. Two-year or short-term degree and diploma programs in automotive, drafting, baking, electrical, refrigeration, printing, machine tool technology. Full/part-time, days and evenings.

Community and technical colleges are listed beginning on page 265.

GLOBE COLLEGE OF BUSINESS
175 East Fifth St., Suite 201
Box 60
St. Paul, MN 55101
(612) 224-4378   Fax—(612) 224-5684

Diploma and degree programs in secretarial, accounting, business administration, medical/veterinary clinical assisting. Days and evenings.

LOWTHIAN COLLEGE
825 Second Ave. So.
Minneapolis, MN 55402
(612) 332-3361   (800) 777-3643

Private college. Associate degrees in fashion merchandising, interior/fashion design. Full and part-time programs, days, evenings, weekends.

MACALESTER COLLEGE
1600 Grand Avenue
St. Paul, MN 55105
(612) 696-6357   Fax—(612) 696-6724

Four-year private liberal arts college. Full and part-time day programs.

METROPOLITAN STATE UNIVERSITY
700 E. Seventh Street
St. Paul, MN 55106
(612) 772-7600

Four year university with campuses in Minneapolis and St. Paul. Day, evening, weekend classes, year-round.

MINNEAPOLIS BUSINESS COLLEGE
1711 W. County Road B
Roseville, MN 55113
(612) 636-7406   (800) 279-5200   Fax—(612) 636-8185

Programs for retailing, travel/hospitality, administrative assistants, accounting, graphic design, and medical assistants. Day classes only.

SCHOOLS & TRAINING CENTERS

MINNEAPOLIS COLLEGE OF ART AND DESIGN
2501 Stevens Ave. So.
Minneapolis, MN 55404
(612) 874-3760

Private professional college of visual arts. Offers day and evening classes, year-round. BFA, MFA degrees.

MINNEAPOLIS DRAFTING SCHOOL
5700 West Broadway
Minneapolis, MN 55428
(612) 535-8843

Private post-secondary technical school. Major programs in architectural or engineering design/drafting. Special programs for college graduates.

MINNESOTA SCHOOL OF BUSINESS
1401 W. 76th Street
Richfield, MN 55423
(612) 861-2000   Fax—(612) 861-5548

Programs in computers, court reporting, office administration, medical, accounting, business. Day and evening classes, year-round.

MINNESOTA SCHOOL OF REAL ESTATE INC.
7148 Shady Oak Road
Eden Prairie, MN 55344
(612) 829-0101   Fax—(612) 829-0801

Preparatory training for real estate, brokers, and appraisers licenses. Day and weekend classes.

NATIONAL COLLEGE
1380 Energy Lane
St. Paul, MN 55108
(612) 644-1265

Private college. Bachelor and associate degrees, diploma programs in business administration, computer information systems, travel and tourism, applied management. Full/part-time, days, evenings, weekends.

Community and technical colleges are listed beginning on page 265.

NATIONAL EDUCATION CENTER
Brown Institute Campus
2225 E. Lake Street
Minneapolis, MN 55407
(612) 721-2481

Two-year art, business, broadcasting and technical college. Day and evening classes, year-round.

NORTHWEST TECHNICAL INSTITUTE
11995 Singletree Lane
Eden Prairie, MN 55344
(612) 944-0080

Two-year private technical institute. Programs in engineering, architectural drafting/design, and CAD technology.

PERSONNEL CONNECTION TRAINING CENTER, INC.
5215 Industrial Blvd.
Edina, MN 55439
(612) 832-0893

Short-term PC training school. Flexible schedules.

RASMUSSEN BUSINESS COLLEGE
12450 Wayzata Blvd.
Minnetonka, MN 55305
(612) 545-2000   Fax—(612) 545-7038

Short-term degree/diploma programs in court reporting, travel, medical records, medical/legal secretary, business, office, and management careers. Day and evening classes. Two metro campuses.

SCHOOL OF COMMUNICATION ARTS
2526 27th Ave. So.
Minneapolis, MN 55406
(612) 721-5357

Private college with majors in advanced computer animation and computer graphics, video, photography, and multimedia.

SCHOOLS & TRAINING CENTERS

UNIVERSITY OF MINNESOTA
Twin Cities Campus
240 Williamson Hall
231 Pillsbury Drive S.E.
Minneapolis, MN 55455
(612) 625-2008   Fax—(612) 626-1693

Four-year public university. Undergraduate, graduate and professional programs. Continuing education and extension divisions. Day, evening and summer classes.

UNIVERSITY OF ST. THOMAS
2115 Summit Avenue
St. Paul, MN 55105
(612) 962-6150

Four-year private liberal arts college. Classes offered year-round. New College offers weekend and evening courses.

NORTHERN MINNESOTA

ARROWHEAD UNIVERSITY CENTER
1515 E. 25th Street
Hibbing, MN 55746
(218) 262-6753   (800) 369-4970

Upper division and master degree credits can be earned through extension classes held at three Community College locations in Hibbing, Grand Rapids and Bemidji.

BEMIDJI STATE UNIVERSITY
1500 Birchmont Drive N.E.
Bemidji, MN 56601-2699
(218) 755-2000   (800) 475-2001

Four-year public university offering degrees in liberal arts. Full and part-time weekday and summer classes.

Community and technical colleges are listed beginning on page 265.

MINNESOTA JOB SEEKER'S SOURCEBOOK

COLLEGE OF ST. SCHOLASTICA
1200 Kenwood Avenue
Duluth, MN 55811
(218) 723-6046   (800) 447-5444

Private liberal arts college with four-year and graduate programs. Full-time, part-time, and summer classes.

CONCORDIA COLLEGE
901 So. 8th Street
Moorhead, MN 56562
(218) 299-3004

Four-year private liberal arts college. Classes full and part-time, summer.

DULUTH BUSINESS UNIVERSITY
412 W. Superior Street
Duluth, MN 55802
(218) 722-3361

Private academic college. Courses of study include accounting, sales/marketing, business management, travel/tourism, office administration. Flexible weekday schedules.

MOORHEAD STATE UNIVERSITY
1104 7th Ave. So.
Moorhead, MN 56503
(218) 236-2011   (800) 593-7246

Four-year public university offers degrees in the liberal arts. Flexible schedules.

UNIVERSITY OF MINNESOTA
Crookston Technical College
Crookston, MN 56716
(218) 281-6510   (800) 232-6466

Four-year public technical college. Day and evening classes offered year-round.

SCHOOLS & TRAINING CENTERS

UNIVERSITY OF MINNESOTA
Duluth Campus
10 University Drive
Duluth, MN 55812
(218) 726-7171   (800) 232-1339

Four-year public university. Undergraduate, graduate, and professional programs. Day, evening, summer classes.

CENTRAL MINNESOTA

COLLEGE OF ST. BENEDICT
37 So. College Avenue
St. Joseph, MN 56374
(612) 363-5308   (800) 544-1489

Private liberal arts college for women. Offers more than 40 majors and pre-professional programs in partnership with St. John's University.

ST. CLOUD BUSINESS COLLEGE
245 37th Ave. No.
St. Cloud, MN 56303
(612) 251-5600

Training in computerized accounting, secretarial, court reporting, sales, travel-business, accounting, word processing programs. Day and evening classes.

ST. CLOUD STATE UNIVERSITY
720 Fourth Ave. So.
St. Cloud, MN 56301
(612) 255-2243   (800) 369-4260.

Public university offers undergraduate and graduate programs in business, education, fine arts, humanities, science, technology, and social sciences.

Community and technical colleges are listed beginning on page 265.

ST. CLOUD HOSPITAL HEALTH CARE SCHOOLS
1406 Sixth Ave. No.
St. Cloud, MN 56303
(612) 255-5632—School of Medical Technology
(612) 255-5619—School of X-Ray Technology

Health care technology training school.

ST. JOHN'S UNIVERSITY
Collegeville, MN 56321
(612) 363-2011   (800) 245-6467

Private liberal arts college for men. Graduate school of theology for men and women.

UNIVERSITY OF MINNESOTA
Morris Campus

105 Behmler Hall
Morris, MN 56267
(612) 589-6035

Four-year public university offering degrees in liberal arts. Full-time.

SOUTHERN MINNESOTA

CARLTON COLLEGE
100 North College
Northfield, MN 55057
(507) 663-4000

Four-year private liberal arts college. Full-time weekday classes.

GUSTAVUS ADOLPHUS COLLEGE
800 W. College Avenue
St. Peter, MN 56082
(507) 933-8000

Four-year private liberal arts college. Full-time weekday classes.

SCHOOLS & TRAINING CENTERS

MANKATO STATE UNIVERSITY
P.O. Box 8400
Mankato, MN 56002
(507) 389-2463

Four-year public university. Degrees and some associate degrees in the liberal arts. Also offers masters and specialist programs. Full and part-time programs. Day, evening, and summer classes.

RASMUSSEN BUSINESS COLLEGE
151 Good Counsel Drive
Mankato, MN 56001
(507) 625-6556

Two-year private business and vocational school offers associate degrees in business. Weekday, evening, and summer classes.

SAINT MARY'S COLLEGE OF MINNESOTA
700 Terrace Heights
Winona, MN 55987
(507) 452-4430

Four-year private liberal arts college. Full-time and part-time, weekday classes.

ST. OLAF COLLEGE
1520 St. Olaf Avenue
Northfield, MN 55057-1098
(507) 646-2222

Four-year private liberal arts college. Full and part-time programs. Weekday and summer classes.

SOUTHWEST STATE UNIVERSITY
1501 State Street
Marshall, MN 56258
(507) 537-7021

Four-year public liberal arts university. Variety of degrees and masters programs. Full and part-time programs. Days, evenings, summer.

Community and technical colleges are listed beginning on page 265.

WINONA STATE UNIVERSITY

P.O. Box 5838
Winona, MN 55987
(507) 457-5000

Four-year public liberal arts university. Variety of degrees and masters programs. Full and part-time, days, evenings, and summer.

WESTERN WISCONSIN

UNIVERSITY OF WISCONSIN

Four-year public university. Undergraduate, graduate, and professional programs. Day, evening, summer classes.

EAU CLAIRE
Eau Claire, WI 54702-4004
(715) 836-5415

LA CROSSE
1725 State Street
La Crosse, WI 54601-9959
(608) 785-8067

RIVER FALLS
112 South Hall
River Falls, WI 54022-5012
(715) 425-3500

STOUT
124 Bowman Hall
Menomonie, WI 54751-0790
(715) 232-1411

SUPERIOR
1800 Grand Avenue
Superior, WI 54880-2980
(715) 394-8230

UNIVERSITY OF WISCONSIN CENTER

Barron County
1800 College Drive
Rice Lake, WI 54868
(715) 234-8176

Community college. Two-year associate degree programs in liberal arts. Full and part-time programs. Day, evening, summer classes.

SCHOOLS & TRAINING CENTERS

COMMUNITY COLLEGES

Community colleges offer a variety of two-year degree programs to meet occupational and educational objectives. Most provide full and part-time options. Day, evening, weekend, and summer classes.

MINNESOTA

ANOKA-RAMSEY COMMUNITY COLLEGE
11200 Mississippi Blvd. N.W.
Coon Rapids, MN 55433
(612) 427-2600

AUSTIN COMMUNITY COLLEGE
1600 N.W. 8th Avenue
Austin, MN 55912
(507) 433-0505   (800) 747-6941

BRAINERD COMMUNITY COLLEGE
501 W. College Drive
Brainerd, MN 56401
(218) 828-2525

CAMBRIDGE COMMUNITY COLLEGE OF ANOKA-RAMSEY
33270 Polk St. N.E.
Cambridge, MN 55008
(612) 689-1536

DULUTH COMMUNITY COLLEGE
1309 Rice Lake Road
Duluth, MN 55811
(218) 723-4796

FERGUS FALLS COMMUNITY COLLEGE
1414 College Way
Fergus Falls, MN 56537
(218) 739-7500

FOND DU LAC COMMUNITY COLLEGE
2101 14th Street
Cloquet, MN 55720
(218) 879-0800

HIBBING COMMUNITY COLLEGE
1515 East 25th Street
Hibbing, MN 55746
(218) 262-6700

INVER HILLS COMMUNITY COLLEGE
8445 College Trail
Inver Grove Heights, MN 55076
(612) 450-8500

ITASCA COMMUNITY COLLEGE
1851 E. Hwy. 169
Grand Rapids, MN 55744
(218) 327-4460

This chapter continues on the following page.

COMMUNITY COLLEGES, cont.

MINNESOTA

LAKEWOOD COMM. COLLEGE
3401 Century Ave. No.
White Bear Lake, MN 55110
(612) 779-3300

MESABI COMMUNITY COLLEGE
9th Ave. W. Chestnut Street
Virginia, MN 55792
(218) 749-7000

MPLS. COMMUNITY COLLEGE
1501 Hennepin Avenue
Minneapolis, MN 55403
(612) 341-7000

NORMANDALE COMM. COLLEGE
9700 France Ave. So.
Bloomington, MN 55431
(612) 832-6320

NORTH HENNEPIN COMMUNITY COLLEGE
7411 85th Ave. No.
Brooklyn Park, MN 55445
(612) 424-0722

NORTHLAND COMM. COLLEGE
1101 Highway One East
Thief River Falls, MN 56701
(218) 681-2181   (800) 628-9918

RAINY-RIVER COMM. COLLEGE
1501 Hwy. 71
International Falls, MN 56649
(218) 285-7722   (800) 456-3996

ROCHESTER COMM. COLLEGE
851 30th Ave. S.E.
Rochester, MN 55904
(507) 285-7210

VERMILION COMM. COLLEGE
1900 E. Camp Street
Ely, MN 55731
(218) 365-7207

WILLMAR COMMUNITY COLLEGE
2021 15th Ave. N.W.
Willmar, MN 56201
(612) 231-5102

WORTHINGTON COMM. COLLEGE
1450 College Way
Worthington, MN 56187
(507) 372-2107   (800) 657-3966

SCHOOLS & TRAINING CENTERS

TECHNICAL COLLEGES

Two-year public technical colleges. Career majors include accounting and business, health and personal services, electronics, manufacturing and transportation. Day, evening, weekend classes, year-round.

MINNESOTA

ALBERT LEA TECHNICAL COLLEGE
2200 Tech Drive
Albert Lea, MN 56007
(507) 373-0656   (800) 333-2584

ALEXANDRIA TECHNICAL COLLEGE
1601 Jefferson Street
Alexandria, MN 56308
(612) 762-0221   (800) 253-9884

ANOKA TECHNICAL COLLEGE
1355 West Highway 10
Anoka, MN 55303
(612) 427-1880

BRAINERD-STAPLES TECHNICAL COLLEGE
300 Quince Street
Brainerd, MN 56401
(218) 828-5344   (800) 247-2574

DAKOTA COUNTY TECHNICAL COLLEGE
1300 E. 145th Street
Rosemount, MN 55068
(612) 423-8301

DULUTH TECHNICAL COLLEGE
2101 Trinity Road
Duluth, MN 55811-3399
(218) 722-2801   (800) 432-2884

HENNEPIN TECHNICAL COLLEGE
1820 North Xenium Lane
Plymouth, MN 55441-3790
(612) 559-3535

HUTCHINSON TECHNICAL COLLEGE
2 Century Avenue
Hutchinson, MN 55350
(612) 587-3636   (800) 222-4424

MANKATO TECHNICAL COLLEGE
1920 Lee Blvd.
North Mankato, MN 56002
(507) 625-3441   (800) 722-9359

MINNEAPOLIS TECHNICAL COLLEGE
1415 Hennepin Ave. So.
Minneapolis, MN 55403
(612) 370-9400

TECHNICAL COLLEGES, cont.

MINNESOTA

MINNESOTA RIVERLAND TECHNICAL COLLEGE
1900 8th Ave. N.W.
Austin, MN 55912
(507) 433-0600   (800) 247-5039

MINNESOTA RIVERLAND TECHNICAL COLLEGE
1225 S.W. Third Street
Faribault, MN 55021
(507) 334-3965   (800) 422-0391

MINNESOTA RIVERLAND TECHNICAL COLLEGE
1926 College View Road S.E.
Rochester, MN 55904
(507) 285-8631   (800) 247-1296

NORTHEAST METRO TECHNICAL COLLEGE
3300 Century Ave. No.
White Bear Lake, MN 55110
(612) 779-5827

NORTHWEST TECH. COLLEGE
905 Grant Ave. S.E.
Bemidji, MN 56601
(218) 759-3200   (800) 942-8324

NORTHWEST TECH. COLLEGE
900 Highway 34 East
Detroit Lakes, MN 56501
(218) 847-1341   (800) 492-4836

NORTHWEST TECHNICAL COLLEGE
Highway 220 No.
P.O. Box 111
East Grand Forks, MN 56721
(218) 773-3441   (800) 451-3441

NORTHWEST TECH. COLLEGE
1900 28th Ave. So.
Moorhead, MN 56560
(218) 236-6277   (800) 426-5603

NORTHWEST TECHNICAL COLLEGE
1301 Highway One East
Thief River Falls, MN 56701
(218) 681-5424   (800) 222-2884

NORTHWEST TECH. COLLEGE
405 Colfax Ave. S.W.
P.O. Box 566
Wadena, MN 56482
(218) 631-3530   (800) 247-2007

PINE TECHNICAL COLLEGE
1000 Fourth Street
Pine City, MN 55063
(612) 629-6764   (800) 521-7463

RANGE TECHNICAL COLLEGE
Hwy. 53
P.O. Box 0648
Eveleth, MN 55734
(218) 744-3302   (800) 345-2884

SCHOOLS & TRAINING CENTERS

RANGE TECHNICAL COLLEGE
2900 E. Beltline
Hibbing, MN 55746
(218) 262-7200   (800) 433-9989

RED WING TECHNICAL COLLEGE
308 Pioneer Road
Red Wing, MN 55066
(612) 388-8271   (800) 657-4849

ST. CLOUD TECHNICAL COLLEGE
1540 Northway Drive
St. Cloud, MN 56303
(612) 654-5000

SAINT PAUL TECHNICAL COLLEGE
235 Marshall Avenue
St. Paul, MN 55102
(612) 221-1300

SOUTHWESTERN TECHNICAL COLLEGE
1011 First St. West
Canby, MN 56220
(507) 223-7252   (800) 658-2535

SOUTHWESTERN TECHNICAL COLLEGE
1593 11th Avenue
Granite Falls, MN 56241
(612) 564-4511   (800) 247-6016

SOUTHWESTERN TECHNICAL COLLEGE
401 West Street
Jackson, MN 56143
(507) 847-3320   (800) 658-2522

SOUTHWESTERN TECHNICAL COLLEGE
1314 No. Hiawatha Avenue
P.O. Box 250
Pipestone, MN 56164
(507) 825-5471   (800) 658-2330

STAPLES TECHNICAL COLLEGE
1830 Airport Road
Staples, MN 56479
(218) 894-1168   (800) 247-6836

WILLMAR TECHNICAL COLLEGE
2101 15th Ave. N.W.
P.O. Box 1097
Willmar, MN 56201
(612) 235-5114   (800) 722-1151

WINONA TECHNICAL COLLEGE
1250 Homer Road
Winona, MN 55987
(507) 454-4600   (800) 372-8164

This chapter continues on the following page.

TECHNICAL COLLEGES, cont.

Two-year public technical college. Career majors in accounting, business, health, personal services, electronics, manufacturing, and transportation. Full and part-time options. Evening, weekend, and summer classes.

WESTERN WISCONSIN

CHIPPEWA VALLEY TECHNICAL COLLEGE
770 Scheidler Road
Chippewa Falls, WI 54729
(715) 723-0261

CHIPPEWA VALLEY TECHNICAL COLLEGE
620 W. Clairemont Avenue
Eau Claire, WI 54701
(715) 833-6200

CHIPPEWA VALLEY TECHNICAL COLLEGE
403 Technology Park Drive East
Menomonie, WI 54751
(715) 232-2685

RIVER FALLS TECHNICAL COLLEGE
P.O. Box 496
River Falls, WI 54022
(715) 425-3301

WESTERN WISCONSIN TECHNICAL COLLEGE
304 No. 6th Street
P.O. Box 908
La Crosse, WI 54602-0908
(608) 785-9200

WISCONSIN INDIANHEAD TECHNICAL COLLEGE
600 No. 21st Street
Superior, WI 54880
(715) 394-6677

Glossary

Career Assessment—The first step in a productive job search. Career assessment is the process of identifying your personal work skills, experience, and employment goals to arrive at a realistic view of your employment potential or satisfaction. Career specialists are trained to assist individuals with this process.

Contract Employment Service—A temporary placement service that hires highly-trained individuals on an assignment basis and provides them to client companies for specified time period or project.

Dislocated Worker—An individual laid off from work through no fault of his or her own either due to economic conditions, or changes in technology. Also includes self-employed individuals hurt by economic conditions, displaced homemakers, and long-term unemployed.

EDWAAA (Economic Dislocation & Worker Adjustment Assistance Act)—Federal funding which helps individuals who lose their jobs through no fault of their own to find employment. Those served include layoff victims, workers not likely to return to their previous jobs or industry, self-employed individuals hurt by the economy, long-term unemployed individuals, and displaced homemakers.

Fee Employment Agency—An employment placement service which can charge fees to the job seeker, to the employer, or to both. In Minnesota, fee employment agencies must be licensed by the state.

Job Bank—A computer data base or other compilation of job vacancies.

JTPA (Job Training Partnership Act)—Federal funding to assist the unemployed or low-income individuals become employed and self-supporting. Special services for Veterans, older workers (55 and over), high school dropouts, and groups with special needs.

Networking—The process of expanding your contacts—friends, relatives, co-workers, business associates, and other acquaintances, etc.—to help you track down a job.

Outplacement—According to the Association of Outplacement Consulting Firms (AOCF), outplacement is a corporate service that helps an employer plan and accomplish terminations or group layoffs. Services also include consultation with the individuals who have been terminated to assist them with articulating their skills and experience in order to plan a job search aimed at finding new employment at the earliest possible date.

Recruitment Publication—Periodicals which list job vacancy ads or listings. Some also contain informational articles on job seeking.

Resume Referral Service—A system in which client or member resumes are kept on file and made available to interested employers.

Search Firm—An employment placement service that recruits individuals for specific jobs which are usually compensated at $50,000 or more. In Minnesota, these firms are not permitted to charge the job seeker a fee.

STRIDE (Success Through Reaching Individual Development & Employment)—A job search program for recipients of AFDC to assist them in finding employment and becoming self-supporting. Services include: coaching in job seeking skills, opportunities for training, support service subsidies and job placement.

Vocational Testing—(Also called "career testing"). A variety of testing instruments, usually administered by a career specialist, which help assess an individual's interests, skills, values, or personality as they relate to a career or vocational choice.

INDEX

BY ORGANIZATION

A

A Plus Typing and Word Processing 89
A.I.O.I.C. Community Job Training Center 51
AAA Employment Agency of Duluth 157
AACC/APS Job Placement Service 170
Ability Resume Services 89
Academy Education Center 254
ACCESS 170
Accountants Exchange, Inc. 147
Accountants Executive Search 147
Accountants On Call 147
Accountants Placement Registry 147
Accounting Action Line 129
Action-Plus Temporary Service 226
Administrative Office Services 95
Advance Personnel Resources 148
Advance/Possis Technical Services 218
Advanced Personnel Placement 148
Aetna Health Plans 129
Affirmative Action Register 162
Affordable Housing Hotline 210, 246
Agri Consultants 148
Agri Search 148
Agro Quality Search Inc. 149

AIA Minnesota 187
Air Jobs Digest 162
Aitkin County Growth Center 231
Albert Lea Technical College 267
Alcoholics Anonymous 196, 201
Alexandria Technical College 113, 267
All-PROfessional Career Management 76
Allen and Associates 76
Alternative Staffing, Inc. 149
American Association of Cereal Chemists 170
American Association of Law Libraries 129
American Federation of Police Operators 136
AARP 253
American Indian OIC 51
American Marketing Association 187
America On-Line 124
American Phytopathological Association 170
American Purchasing Society 171
American Society For Mechanical Engineers 187
American Society of Women Accountants 188

MINNESOTA JOB SEEKER'S SOURCEBOOK

Andcor Human Resources   218
Andrea, Richard E., Ph.D   83
Anishinabe Council of Job Developers   51
Anoka County   129
Anoka County Job Training Center   40
Anoka Technical College   267
Anoka-Ramsey Community College   101, 265
Apartment Search   248
APICS—Educational Society For Resource Management   187
Apple Valley Counseling Clinic   77
Area Information and Referral Service   204
Army Employer Network   170
Arrowhead Community Economic Assistance Corp.   235
Arrowhead Economic Opportunity Agency   64, 199
Arrowhead University Center   259
ARTJOB   162
Associated Career Services, Inc.   77
Association Trends Magazine   173
Athletic Employment Weekly   162
Augsburg College   101, 129, 255
Austin Community College   116, 265

B

BRS After Dark   124
Bankers Systems   130
Barr Engineering   130
Bemidji OIC   65
Bemidji State University   110, 259
Bernard Haldane Associates   77
Beth El Synagogue   177
Bi-County Community Action   199
Bilek Consulting   77
Blue Cross/Blue Shield of Minnesota   130
Blue Earth County Information and Referral   203
Brainerd Community College   110, 265
Brainerd-Staples Technical College   110, 267
Breckenridge Business Center   231
Briarwood Consultants   86
Bright Search/Professional Staffing   149
Brogan, Kathleen   91
Bulletin Board System (BBS)   125
Burger & Burger Creative Services   99
Burnet Relocation Management   246
Business Incubation Center   239
Business Office Support Services   89

C

Calvary Lutheran Church   177
Cambridge Community College   265
Cannon Business Industrial Center   231
Career America Connection   130
Career Centers, Inc.   149
Career Connections   97, 163
Career Dynamics   78
Career Opportunities Preparation For Employment   51
Career Placement Registry   171
Career Resources/Staffing Resources   160
Caritas Family Services   201, 213
Carlson School of Management   106
Carlton College   262
Carver County Employment and Training Center   40
Carver-Scott Educational Cooperative   54, 56
Catholic Charities   201
CDI Corporation — North Central   218
Cedarwood Secretarial Service   99
Cenacle Retreat House   177
Centennial United Methodist Church   177
Center For Asians and Pacific Islanders   52

INDEX

Center For Career Change 52, 171, 253
Center For Counseling and Stress Management 78
Center for Senior Citizen's Education 253
Central Cultural Chicano Inc. 52
Central Lutheran Church 178
Century Design Inc. 219
CERNET 130
Chambers of Commerce
  Bemidji 188, 250
  Duluth 188, 250
  Eau Claire, WI 188, 251
  Faribault 188, 250
  Grand Rapids 188, 250
  Greater Minneapolis 54, 247
  Hibbing 188, 250
  International Falls 250
  La Crosse, WI 188, 251
  Mankato 188, 250
  Menomonie, WI 189, 251
  Moorhead 189, 250
  Owatonna 189, 250
  Rochester 189, 250
  St. Cloud 189, 250
  St. Paul 249
  Superior, WI 189, 251
Child Care Resource & Referral Line 196, 247
Children's Hospital 208
Children's On Call 208
Chippewa Valley Technical College 120, 270
Choices — SE Minnesota 70
Christ Presbyterian Church 178
Christ The King Church 178
Chrysalis 197
City Line 131
City of Minneapolis 131
City of St. Paul 131
City Secretary Inc. 95

CityBusiness 233
CLUES 52
COBRA 207
College of Associated Arts 255
College of St. Benedict 114, 261
College of St. Catherine 101, 132, 255
College of St. Scholastica 111, 260
Colonial Church of Edina 178
Community Clinic Consortium 208
Community Jobs 163
Community Volunteer Service of St. Croix Valley Area 241
Complete Career Services 85
CompuServe 124
Compu-Search Inc. 150
Computer Personnel R Partners 150
Computer Services Plus 99
Concordia College 255, 260
Consolidated Services 219
Consumer Credit Counseling Services 211, 212, 213, 214
Contact 203
Contract Employment Weekly 163
Corporate Information Technology Services 89
Corporate Report Minnesota 233
Corporate Resources Professional Placement 150
Craig Group International 78
Crisis Connection 197
Crookston Technical College 260
Crystal Evangelical Free Church 179
Current Jobs For Graduates 163

D

Dacon Engineering and Service Company, Inc. 219
Dahlberg 132
Dakota County 132
Dakota County Employment and Training Center 40, 179

MINNESOTA JOB SEEKER'S SOURCEBOOK

Dakota County Technical College 101, 267
Damark International 132
Dashe & Thomson Technical Writing Consultants 219
Datacard Job Posting Hotline 132
Data-Star 124
David D. Cady and Associates 78
Day Works 237
Daytons 132
Delacore Resources 158
Deluxe Corporation 132
Design Resume and Page Layout 97
Development Resource Group 220
Developmental Resources, Inc. 79
Dialog 124
Diane's Secretarial Service 93
Distinction In Design 220
Division of Rehabilitation Services 45
Dobbs Pro Staff 227
Dodge Business Research Consulting 126
Donovan & Associates 85
Douglas Associates 79
Dow Jones News Retrieval 124
Duluth Business University 260
Duluth Community College 111, 265
Duluth Job Training Center 43
Duluth Technical College 111
Dunwoody Institute 255

E

East Side Neighborhood Service 53, 179
Eden Prairie School District 133
Edina Realty Relocation Services 247
Editorial Freelance Association 133
Educatonal Opportunity Center 53
Electronic Ink 95
Ells Personnel 150
Empire Builder Center 231

Employee Development Services of Wisconsin 99
Employment Action Center 53
Employment and Training Center 67
Employment Plus 96
Employment Review 164
Employment Specialists 160
Engineering Resources of Minnesota 220
Enrollment Options Hotline 246
Environmental Career Opportunities 164
Environmental Opportunities 164
ESP Software Services, Inc. 220
ESP Systems Professionals, Inc. 151
Esquire Search Ltd. 151
Ethiopians In Minnesota, Inc. 54
Exec-U-Net 164
Execu-Tech Search, Inc. 151
Executive Suites On First 96
Expanded Horizons 54
Express Personnel Services 158, 227

F

Fairmont Business Development Center 231
Fairview Southdale Hospital 133
Family & Children's Service of the Minneapolis Metro Area 212
Family Resource Center Helpline 201
Family Service Inc. 51, 212
Fare Share 210
Faribault Senior High School 116
Federal Career Opportunities 165, 170
Federal Cartridge 133
Federal Jobs Digest 165
Federal Jobs Hotline 133
Federal Reserve Bank of Minneapolis 134
Federal Women's Program 134
Fergus Falls Community College 114, 265

INDEX

Fine Line Resume Service 90
First Call For Help
  East Metro 197
  Grand Rapids 199
  La Crosse 205
  Northfield 203
  St. Cloud 200
  West Metro 197
First Evangelical Lutheran Church 179
Fitzgerald Resume Writing and Career Counseling 90
Flatley Services 221
Flexwork 65, 67
Fluoroware 134
Fond Du Lac Community College 111, 265
40 Plus of Minnesota 54, 180
Functional Industries Inc. 68

G

Gary Johnson & Associates 79
Gay and Lesbian Helpline 197
General Mills 134
Genesis Business Centers Ltd. 231
GENIE 124
George Konik Associates, Inc. 221
Gibbs Temporary Employment Service 228
Gillette Company 134
Ginsberg Psychological Service 85
Gisleson Writing Services 90
Globe College of Business 256
Grace Lutheran Church 180
Graco 134
Greater Minneapolis Chamber of Commerce 54, 247
Green Thumb, Inc. 65, 68, 71
Green Tree Financial Corporation 134
Gustavus Adolphus College 262

H

H R Services 151
H. L. Yoh/Salem Technical Services 223
Hamline University 102, 135
Hastings Senior High School 116
Hazelden Information Center 196
Health Risk Management 135
Healthcare Recruiters of Minnesota 152
Healthspan Medformation 209
Heartland Community Action Agency 201
Henderson Business Center 231
Hennepin County 135
Hennepin County Bar Association 152, 211
Hennepin County Dept. of Training & Employment Assistance 41
Hennepin Technical College 102, 267
Hibbing Community College 112, 265
Hibbing Volunteer Council 242
Hill-Burton Facilities 208
HIRED 55, 180
Hoffman Engineering 135
Holy Name of Jesus Church 181
Homebased & Small Business Network 233
Honeywell 135
Hopkins Adult Career Center 102
HRP of Minnesota 189
HSI Crisis Clinics 198
HTC Employment and Training Programs 55
Hubbard Broadcasting 135
Human Development Center 199
Hutchinson Technical College 267

I

IBM 135
IDI Corporation 221
IDS 136

MINNESOTA JOB SEEKER'S SOURCEBOOK

Independent School District 281   136
INFORM   126
Information Management Systems, Inc.   90
Inroads—Mpls./St.Paul   55
Insurance Talent/Business Talent   152
Intelaction Inc., Career Services   79
Inter County Community Council   199
International Career Employment Opportunities   165
International Employment Gazette   165
Inver Hills Community College   265
Itasca Community College   112, 265
ITT Consumer Finance   136

J

J.O.B.   166
James J. Hill Reference Library   126
Jewish Vocational Service   56
Job Bank USA   171
Job Exchange Inc.   172
Job Information Letter   166
Job Placement   171
Job Placement Center   56
Job Service   36
Job Service Job Bank   172

K

Kelly Encore Temporary Services   221
Kelly Temporary Services
  Rochester   228
  St.Cloud   227
KiNexus   172
Kinko's Copy Center   96
Korn/Ferry International   152
Kreofsky and Associates   153
Kuller-Fleming and Associates   153
Kurenitz & Associates   80

L

L & S Office Services   91
L.D.A. Enterprises   80
La Oportunidad   56
Lake Country Information Line   202
Lakewood Community College   103, 266
Land O' Lakes/Cenex   136
Lao Family Community of Minnesota   56
Lee Marsh and Associates   153
Leech Lake Retail Center   231
Leiders Employment Service   159
Lexis   124
Liberty Diversified Industries   136
Life Development Counseling   86
Life Dimensions, Inc.   80
Life-Work Planning Center   71
Lifeworks   103
Linda's Pageworks   93
Little Six Casino   137
Living Guide   248
Loftus Brown-Wescott, Inc.   80
Loring Nicollet-Bethlehem Community Center, Inc.   57
Love Lines, Inc.   198
Lowthian College   256
Lutheran Social Services   65, 202, 213
L—J Enterprises   96

M

Macalester College   103, 137, 256
Mainstay, Inc.   71
Management Recruiters   153
Management Recruiters of Rochester   159
Mankato Manufacturing Incubator   231
Mankato State University   263
Mankato Technical College   267
Manpower Temporary Services   226, 227, 228, 229

INDEX

Market Share Inc.   81
Marquette Bank   137
Marriott   137
Mary Erickson & Associates   153
Masterson Personnel Inc.   154
May We Help II   94
Mayo Foundation   137
McGladrey and Pullen   157
McGlynn Bakery   138
Medsearch Corp.   154
Meeting Planners International   189
Mesabi Community College   266
Metropolitan Council Data Center   125, 248
Metropolitan Economic Development Association   234
Metropolitan Financial Corporation   138
Metropolitan Senior Federation   171
Metropolitan State University   104, 256
Metropolitan Transit Commission   138
Midtown Secretarial Services   98
Midwest Direct Marketing Asso.   190
Midwest Farmworker Employment & Training, Inc.   68
Miller Dwan Medical Center Crisis Line   200
Minneapolis Age and Opportunity Center   57
Minneapolis Business College   256
Minneapolis Children's Medical Center   138
Minneapolis College of Art and Design   257
Minneapolis Community College   104, 266
Minneapolis Drafting School   257
Minneapolis Employment and Training Program   41
Minneapolis Post Office   138
Minneapolis Technical College   267
Minneapolis Urban League   57

Minnegasco   138
Minnesota Broadcasters Association   190
Minnesota Business Breakfasts   190
Minnesota Business Opportunities   233
Minnesota Career Information System   125
Minnesota Career Opportunities   166
Minnesota Community Colleges   138
Minnesota Department of Education   125, 246
Minnesota Department of Human Rights   211
Minnesota Entrepreneurs' Club   232
Minnesota Food Shelf Association   210
Minnesota Human Development Consultants, Inc.   81
Minnesota Mainstream   57
Minnesota Mutual Life Insurance   139
Minnesota Project Outreach   232
Minnesota Recreation and Park Association   190
Minnesota Riverland Technical College   117, 268
Minnesota School of Business   257
Minnesota School of Real Estate Inc.   257
Minnesota Senior Federation   253
Minnesota Small Business Development Centers   232
Minnesota Society of Certified Public Accountants   191
Minnesota Society of Professional Engineers   191
Minnesota Telecommunications Asso.   139, 191
Minnesota Valley Action Council, Inc.   71, 203
Minnesota Ventures   233
Minnesota Women In The Trades   139, 191
MinnesotaCare   207
Minnetonka Adult Career Center   104

Moorhead State University   260
MSI Insurance   137
Multifoods   139

N

National and Federal Legal Employment Report   166
National Asso. For Interpretation   133
National Asso. For The Self-Employed   233
National Asso. of Chiefs of Police   136
National Asso. of Social Workers   192
National Business Employment Weekly   167
National College   257
National Computer Systems   139
National Contract Managers Asso.   172
National Education Center   258
National Engineering Resources   222
National Society For Performance and Instruction   192
Nationwide Jobs In Dietetics   167
NCMA Job Bank Referral Service   172
New Chance   58
NewsNet   124
Nexis   124
Non-Traditional Employment For Women   66
Normandale Community College   104, 266
North Hennepin Community College   105, 266
North Star Employment   158
Northeast Entrepreneur Fund, Inc.   235
Northeast Metro Technical College   105, 268
Northeast Minnesota Office of Job Training   43
Northern States Power   139
Northland Business Services   94
Northland Community College   266

Northland Volunteer Council, Inc.   242
Northstar Personnel   226
Northwest Airlines   139
Northwest Health Club   140
Northwest Technical College   114, 258, 268
Northwest Technical Institute   258
Northwestern National Life   140
Norwest Bank   140

O

Office of The Blind, Wisconsin   45
Ojibwa Employment & Training Center   66
Olmsted Community Action Program   72
Olsten's Staffing Service   157
Omni/Officeplus   91
On-Line Career Center Inc.   173
Opportunity Training Center, Inc.   68
Outplacement International Minnesota   81
Owatonna Incubator Inc.   231
Owatonna Senior High School   117

P

Pace Inc.   140
Pathfinder Personnel Services, Inc.   81
Pax Christi Catholic Community   181
Pencraft Resume Service   91
Personal Profile Services   91
Personal Touch Office Services   98
Personnel Decisions, Inc.   82
Personnel Unlimited Executive Search   160
Perspectives Media Communications   92
Perspectives, Inc.   198
Peterson Typing Service   98
Pfaffly Personnel Resources   154

INDEX

Phillips Community Development Corp. 58
Pillsbury Company 140
Pillsbury Neighborhood Services, Inc. 58, 181
Pine Technical College 114, 268
Pinnacle Search Ltd. 154
Piper Jaffray 140
Prairie 5 Community Action Council, Inc. 202
Printing Industry of Minnesota Inc. 192
Private Industry Council 5 69
Private Industry Council—Austin 72
Processus 85
Prodigy 124
Professional Ass. For Occupational Therapists In Minnesota 192
Professional Business Services 160
Professional Career Alternatives 82
Professional Profiles 92
Professional Typing 96
Programming Alternatives Inc. 222
Project Self-Sufficiency 58
Project Soar 66
Prototype Career Services 82
Prudential Insurance Company 141
Public Relations Society of America 193
Public Sector Job Bulletin 167
Putting It All Together 59

Q

Quality Temp 227, 229

R

Radisson Hotel South 141
Rainy River Community College 112, 266
Ramsey County 141
Ramsey County Job Training Program 41
Ramsey County OIC 59
Range Technical College 112, 268, 269
Rasmussen Business College 258, 263
Red Wing Technical College 269
Regional Development Commissions 235, 236, 238
Resource Publishing Group Inc. 82
Resume Specialists 92
Resume-On-File 173
Retirement Enterprises, Inc. 222
RFA/Minnesota Engineering 222
RISE, Inc. 59
River Falls Technical College 270
Robert Half International Inc. 155
Rochester Career Counseling Center, 86
Rochester Community College 117, 266
Rollerblade 141
Roseville Area Ind. School District 105
Roth Young Executive Recruiters 155
Rural Employment Placement Project 69
Rural Minnesota CEP, Inc. 67, 70
RWJ and Associates 159

S

Saint Mary's College of Minnesota 263
Saint Paul Area Chamber of Commerce 249
Saint Paul Technical College 105, 269
Sales and Marketing Executives 193
Sales Consultants of Minneapolis 155
Sathe & Associates 155
SBA Small Business Answer Desk 233
School of Communication Arts 258
Science Museum of Minnesota 141
SCORE 234, 237, 238, 239
Scott County Human Services 42
Search Resources, Inc. 226
Secretary On Call 94
Senior Design Corporation 223
Senior Linkage Line 198
Signature Resumes 98

Snelling and Snelling 155
Social Service Jobs 167
Society for Marketing Professional Services 193
Society for Technical Communications 193
Sorensen & Associates, Inc. 83
Source Services 156
Source Tech Corporation 223
South Central Technical College 118
Southeast Minnesota Information and Referral 204
Southeast Minnesota Job Training Center 72
Southeast Minnesota Private Industry Council, Inc. 72
Southeastern Minnesota Initiative Fund 239
Southwest Minnesota Private Industry Council 73
Southwest Opportunity Council 204
Southwest State University 118, 263
Southwestern Technical College 119, 269
Special Libraries Association 142
St. Alphonsus Church 181
St. Andrew Lutheran Church 182
St. Cloud Area Economic Development Partnership 236
St. Cloud Business College 261
St. Cloud Hospital Health Care Schools 262
St. Cloud State University 115, 261
St. Cloud Technical College 115, 269
St. Croix Technical 223
St. Edwards Catholic Church 182
St. Francis Regional Medical Center 208
St. Gerard's Church 182
St. James Lutheran Church 182
St. Joan of Arc Catholic Church 183
St. John Neumann Catholic Church 183
St. John's University 115, 262
St. Louis County Social Services 200
St. Olaf College 118, 263
St. Paul Employment & Training Center 42
St. Paul Labor Studies and Resource Center 59
St. Paul Pioneer Press 142
St. Paul Post Office 141
St. Paul Ramsey Medical Center 142, 209
St. Paul Urban League 60
St. Steven's Episcopal Church 183
Standby Secretaries, Inc. 92
Staples Technical College 269
Star Tribune 142
Star Tribune Fax Service 249
Star Tribune Fonahome 249
Start Renting 248
State of Minnesota 142
State Services For The Blind and Visually Handicapped, Minnesota 45
Stearns-Benton Employment & Training Council 43
Steffen Career Services, Inc. 83
Stepping Stones 69
Strom Engineering Corporation 224
Suburban Pathways 60
SuperValu 142
Superior Career Professionals 92
Superior Senior Services, Inc. 224
Sysco Minnesota 142

T

T. H. Hunter, Inc. 156
TAD Technical Services Corp. 224
TAPS 60, 184
T.I.E.S. 174
Target Headquarters 143
Tech Central Inc. 224

INDEX

Technical Career Placements Inc. 159, 229
Technical Employment 168
Techniforce 225
Techpower, Inc. 225
Tel Law 211
Tel-Med 209
Tele-Health 209
Temple Israel 184
The Arthur Group 83
The Career Bridge, Inc. 84
The City, Inc. 60
The Collaborative 233
The Crisis Line 202
The Franklin Business Center, 231
The Job Seeker 168
The Mazzitelli Group Ltd. 156
The Meredith Company of Minnesota 84
The National Ad Search 168
The New Professional Group 173
The Nycor Group 225
The Personnel Connection Training Center, Inc. 258
The Position Report 168
The Practice of Kinlein 86
The Recruiting Group 156
The Resume Place 93
The Resume Shop 93
The Secretarian 97
The Volunteer Connection 243
The Work Connection 228, 229
Tri-County Community Action Program 236, 237
Tri-Valley Opportunity Council 200
Turnaround 73
Twin Cities Business Monthly 233
Twin Cities Computer Network 174
Twin Cities Employment Weekly 168
Twin Cities Men's Center 184
Twin Cities OIC 61
Twin Cities Personnel Asso. 143, 194
Twin Cities Quality Assurance Asso. 194
Twin Cities Tourism Information Line 249
Twin City Purchasing Management Association 184, 194

U

U.S. Department of Veterans Affairs 44
U.S. Small Business Administration 233, 234
United Cambodian Asso. of Minnesota 61
United For Excellence Inc. 143
United Hospital 143
United Way of St. Cloud Area 243
United Way's Volunteer Center 241
University Health Line 209
University of Minnesota 143
   Crookston 113, 260
   Duluth 113, 261
   Morris 262
   Twin Cities 259
      College of Agriculture 106
      College of Biological Sciences 107
      College of Education 107
      College of Human Ecology 107
      College of Liberal Arts 108
      Dept. of Counseling, Continuing Education & Extension 106
      Hubert H. Humphrey Institute of Public Affairs 108
      Institute of Technology 108
      University Counseling and Consulting Services 109
      Vocational Assessment Clinic 109
University of Minn. Dental Clinic 209
University of St. Thomas 109, 143, 253, 259
University of St. Thomas Enterprise Center 231
University of Wisconsin 120, 121. 264

MINNESOTA JOB SEEKER'S SOURCEBOOK

University of Wisconsin Center   264
University Technology Center, Inc.   231

V

Vaughn Communications   143
Vermilion Community College   266
Vet Center   61
Veterans Employment and Training Service   44
Veterans Re-Employment Rights   44
Video Unlimited   94
Voluntary Action Center   243
Voluntary Action Center of The St. Paul Area, Inc.   242
Voluntary Action Center of United Way   243
Volunteer Services   244
Volunteer Services of Carlton County   244
Volunteers Working Together   244

W

Walker Art Center   144
Washington County   144
Washington County Job Training Center   42
Wausaw Insurance Company   144
Wayzata Community Church   185
WCCO Television   144
West Central Minnesota Communities Action   203
West Central Wisconsin Community Action Agency   205
West Central Wisconsin Private Industry Council   74
Western Community Action   204
Western Technical Services   225
Western Wisconsin Technical College   270
Whitney & Associates, Inc.   157

Wilder Foundation   144
Willmar Community College   266
Willmar Technical College   269
Wings   61, 70
Winona Dept. of Jobs and Training   44
Winona State University   119, 264
Winona Technical College   119, 269
Wisconsin Division of Vocational Rehabilitation   46
Wisconsin Green Thumb, Inc.   74
Wisconsin Indianhead Technical College   121, 270
WML   97
Women Achieving New Directions   62
Women In Communications, Inc.   194
Women In Transition   62
Women's Employment Resource Center   62
WomenVenture   62, 185, 234
Wooddale Church   185
Word Processing of Duluth   95
Work/Life Transitions   84
Working Options   84
Working Opportunities for Women   63
Worthington Community College   266

Y

Young Dads   63
Youth Employment & Training   63
Youth Employment Project, Inc.   73
Youth Express   63

ORDER FORM

Did you borrow this book?

Here's how to order your copy of the Minnesota Job Seeker's Sourcebook.

"BEST ALL-AROUND BOOK"
Minnesota Book Achievement Merit Award

Telephone orders: Call (612) 545-5980.
Please have VISA or MasterCard ready.

Postal orders: Mail a copy of this order form with payment to:
Resource Publishing Group, Inc.
P. O. Box 573, Hopkins, MN 55343

❑ Please enter my order for _____ copies of the Minnesota Job Seeker's Sourcebook at $17.95 each.

NAME_____
ORGANIZATION_____
ADDRESS_____
CITY _____ STATE_____ ZIP _____
PHONE (____) _____

SALES TAX:
Add 6.5% sales tax for books shipped to a Minnesota address.
If you are exempt from sales tax, please attach a copy of your exemption certificate.

SHIPPING:
Add $4.00 for the first book and $1.50 for each additional book.

PAYMENT:

❑ Check: Amount enclosed $ _____
❑ Credit Card: ❑ VISA ❑ MasterCard

CARD NUMBER _____
NAME ON CARD _____ EXP. DATE _____
SIGNATURE_____